Gospel Women
at the United Nations

Gospel Women at the United Nations

Handmaids of the Sacred Heart
Doing Public Theology

MARGARET D. SCOTT

WIPF & STOCK · Eugene, Oregon

GOSPEL WOMEN AT THE UNITED NATIONS
Handmaids of the Sacred Heart Doing Public Theology

Copyright © 2019 Margaret D. Scott. All rights reserved. Except for brief quotations in critical publications or reviews, no part of this book may be reproduced in any manner without prior written permission from the publisher. Write: Permissions, Wipf and Stock Publishers, 199 W. 8th Ave., Suite 3, Eugene, OR 97401.

Wipf & Stock
An Imprint of Wipf and Stock Publishers
199 W. 8th Ave., Suite 3
Eugene, OR 97401

www.wipfandstock.com

PAPERBACK ISBN: 978-1-5326-6581-3
HARDCOVER ISBN: 978-1-5326-6582-0
EBOOK ISBN: 978-1-5326-6583-7

Manufactured in the U.S.A. FEBRUARY 26, 2019

To my Sisters, the Handmaids of the Sacred Heart of Jesus, and all passionate women religious or not, who care about the poor and the planet enough to spend their time and their energy protecting them.

Contents

Acknowledgments | ix

Introduction | 1

Chapter 1   The What, Why, and How of Public Theology | 5
Chapter 2   Public Theology and Catholic Social Teaching | 17
Chapter 3   The History, the Mandate, and the Working of the United Nations | 44
Chapter 4   Non-Governmental Organizations (NGOs) and the United Nations | 70
Chapter 5   Handmaids of the Sacred Heart of Jesus | 85
Chapter 6   UNANIMA International and its aims | 102
Conclusion Handmaids and the UN | 113

Glossary | 125
Bibliography | 131

Acknowledgments

MY GRATITUDE GOES TO the Lutheran Theological Seminary in Philadelphia, where I discovered public theology and which afforded me the time and space to research it for my doctoral thesis; to Dr. David Grafton who was my patient and inspirational guide on this journey; and to Fr Dan Joyce, SJ, whose idea it was in the first place.

Introduction

MY DOCTORAL THESIS, "GOSPEL Women at the UN," is about passion: passion for Jesus Christ, for the poor, and for the planet. It tells the story of a small group of Catholic Sisters, the Handmaids of the Sacred Heart of Jesus, and how their concern for the underprivileged and for human rights developed from teaching poor girls in the basement of a convent to working for social justice and systemic change at the United Nations. Their aim: to engage, at the crossroads of world affairs, with the social issues embedded in contemporary society; and to do public theology.

The context for this story consists, firstly, of a brief description of the emergence and definitions—the "what, why, and how"—of public theology, with its intent to bring God's tenderness and compassion to the public square. This is followed, in chapter 2, by a reflection on the corpus of the social teaching of the Catholic Church, beginning with Pope Leo XII's foundational document, *Rerum Novarum,* and moving across three centuries to the latest encyclical, penned by Francis I, *Laudato Si'*, as examples of public theology in practice.

In the following four chapters, I introduce the protagonists in this story: the United Nations organisation; the non-governmental organisations (NGOs) who partner with the UN in its commitment to human rights and sustainable development; UNANIMA International, a coalition of Sisters with NGO status at the UN; and lastly, as mentioned above, the Handmaids of the Sacred Heart of Jesus, of which I am a member. The Handmaids recently joined

UNANIMA in order to further our determination to be "gospel women" engaging in public theology. The interaction between these protagonists and the interweaving of the strands that run through the tapestry of their interconnected stories, as they work together on behalf of social justice and human rights, form the central core of this book. Together they pulsate to the rhythm of the common good and the basic human values that provide a meeting place for hearts and minds.

The history of the UN, from its birth in 1945 to its role in international politics today, necessarily recalls the blend of high ideals and lofty ambitions set out in the founding charter that is all too often tempered by stark political realities. I have highlighted both its successes and its failures, and also its politicization and the conflicts of interest among its member states. These conflicts limit its effectiveness, above all, as far as the protection of human rights is concerned. Examples abound and I have tried to lend a little drama and excitement to the narrative with some blow-by-blow personal eyewitness accounts of the wrangling and infighting.

Chapter 4 is dedicated to the growing host of NGOs that work alongside the UN, bringing with them passion, energy, and commitment. They make an important contribution to the promotion and protection of human rights and humanitarian principles and are, potentially, catalysts for change. Armed with consultative status, they are active in a wide range of human rights issues at the UN, lobbying member states, circulating documents, and speaking at UN subcommittee meetings and other groups. The NGO community in New York includes many religious—or faith-based—RNGOs. While all world religions have their representatives, the majority are Christian groups, including many Catholic religious orders. As followers of Jesus Christ identified with his mission, their aspiration is to bring the gospel message to the UN.

UNANIMA International is just such an RNGO. Its story is that of a coalition of Catholic Sisters, determined to bring a feminine spirit to the UN and to take the cause of the weakest and the least, particularly woman and girls, to the public square. Born in 2001, its membership has grown over the years and its outreach

Introduction

has increased until now it numbers some 22,000 Sisters who work at the grassroots in 82 different countries. Its mission statement has evolved in response to the needs of international society and changing world politics. A member of several key subcommissions at the UN, UNANIMA now advocates on behalf of women and children, particularly those living in poverty, victims of human trafficking, immigrants, refugees, and the homeless, as well as the welfare of the planet. The Handmaids of the Sacred Heart of Jesus became one of its most recent members when in 2012, we made a conscious decision that the poor and the planet could not wait any longer. Action was needed immediately.

The Handmaids of the Sacred Heart of Jesus, a group of women in love with Jesus Christ, whose hearts beat to the rhythm of the cry of the poor and the wounded earth, are the main protagonists in this story. Although ours is a tale of adventure and conflict since our founding in 1877, I have chosen to focus on the life of our foundress, St. Raphaela Mary (1850–1925), and her legacy to the Sisters of love for the poor and the vulnerable and a desire for social reform. That heritage has kept pace with the expansion of the Sisters, who now live and work in 28 different countries ministering mainly to the poor and suffering, while always moving on in step with the growth of the social teaching of the Catholic Church and the emergence of public theology. It has been a natural progression for us to develop from trying to educate poor children out of poverty to combating structural sin in the face of intolerable social and economic inequalities, as well as to be creative in our options for the poor by finding a new place and a new way to serve them: at the UN.

I bring this story to an end—an open end—by looking to the future and its yet-unwritten chapters. It is an uncertain geopolitical future, which challenges the creativity of all the protagonists. At the same time, the UN's outdated structure and unwieldy organizations demand urgent reform. It faces increasing and almost impossible new demands while depending on unreliable funding. The UN is in perpetual political transition. Now a new Cold War, radical nationalism and unilateralism, together with a global shift of power towards the South and the East, loom on the horizon of our post-9/11 world.

These are some of the issues that confront the new Secretary General and the member states of the UN. These same issues also confront UNANIMA International and the Handmaids of the Sacred Heart in their work at the UN, and perhaps would even at a new, a different UN. But what will not change is the commitment of the Handmaids of the Sacred Heart to the legacy of St. Raphaela to social justice. Rather, it will be enhanced; enriched by the new facets that emerge as we respond to the changing needs of our fragile world and confront the challenges that doing public theology poses.

Public theology's role today is not to indulge in "abstract theorizing or eloquent indignation"[1] but to bring God's tenderness and care into the public square, to transform indifference into solidarity, and to disrupt the dominant social and economic narratives that cause and maintain inequality and marginalization. Pope Francis is doing public theology every day. The Handmaids of the Sacred Heart want to do it too. Our identity and our mission will continue to be that of gospel women in love with Jesus Christ, called to protect the planet and the poor and to be passionate practitioners of public theology at the United Nations.

Enjoy our story.

---

1. Francis. "Address to World Meeting of Popular Movements." Santa Cruz, Bolivia (July 9, 2015). https://www.en.radiovaticana.va/news/2015/07/10/Pope_francis_at_world_meeting_of_popular_movements/1157291.

Chapter 1

The What, Why, and How of Public Theology

According to the *Journal of Public Theology,* Pope Francis's address to Congress was a "Major Public Theological Event." The rationale given for this statement: "No religious figure has so strongly influenced the public moral sphere recently in this country as Pope Francis in this major address to Congress."[1]

What is a "public theological event"? And what is "public theology" or "theology in the public square" that characterizes such an event? Both are terms that are prominent in the abundant literature relating to public theology. However, in that growing corpus of books and articles, the exact meaning of the term public theology is a subject of debate. Definitions of public theology are many and varied, and its forms numerous and diverse. In addition, the concept of public theology has developed, unfolding over time. Its "public" contexts have been transformed by globalization and technology. New problems and issues emerge, generated by a rapidly changing global landscape with its geo-economic, political, and cultural upheavals. The term has also undergone a gradual shift of

---

1. Kim, Sebastian. *Online Journal of Public Theology.* September 24, 2015. http://www.pubtheo.com/page.asp?pid=2033 (no longer accessible).

emphasis from the relevance of religious values and its critique of society to concern for the "common good" to "engagement on behalf of social justice in the age of empire."[2] Public theology is about ethical issues and human rights, about the poor, and about trying to articulate the meaning of the gospel in public life. Similarly, the practitioners of public theology have both increased and diversified to include the church, Christian communities, theologians, writers, poets, movie stars, athletes, and other passionate people who care deeply. Examples are many and well-known: the rock star Bono, together with all the members of his band U2, wants to eradicate poverty; Angeline Jolie, who as well as supporting 27 causes is a special envoy for the United Nations High Commissioner for Refugees; Tom Hanks with his wide range of charities; and Andre Agassi, who founded Athletes for Hope, to name just a few. Public theology's forum has extended from American social, economic, and political life to global issues in the international community. And, while I intend to speak about "public theology" in a Catholic context, it is essentially and intensely ecumenical, with what Gerard Mannion describes as "emerging forms of interreligious public theologizing."[3] So much so that, as Mannion goes on to say: "one soon realizes that in reality the term is a vast umbrella concept for a diverse array of methods, issues, challenges, and hermeneutical tools and approaches themselves."[4]

Indeed, a closer look at a spectrum of alternative definitions of the term "public theology" indicates that there is no universal definition. In *Models of Public Theology*, the Brazilian theologian Eneida Jacobsen reminds us that: "In 1978, Charles Strain notes that 'as with all initial efforts to specify the parameters of a particular genre, the definition of the term varies from person to person.'"[5] Two decades later, Max Stackhouse claims that the

---

2. Slessarev-Jamir, Helene. "The Mission of Public Theology in an Age of Empire." *Sage Journals* (2006) Abstract. http://mis.sagepub.com/content/34/1/31.

3. Mannion, "A Brief Genealogy of Public Theology," 122.

4. Mannion, "A Brief Genealogy of Public Theology," 122.

5. Jacobsen, *Models of Public Theology*, 8.

term "public theology" is in dispute and has taken several forms. In 2007, Dirk Smit came to the conclusion that "there exists no single and authoritative meaning of public theology and no single normative way of doing public theology."[6] Jacobsen adds that Harold Breitenberg, in *To Tell the Truth: Will The Real Public Theology Please Stand Up?*, reaches the following conclusion: "in short, the more I read about public theology, the less clear I am that everyone engaged in discussion and debate about it is talking about the same thing."[7]

Perhaps so, but exploring the term "public theology" in the work of a representative sample of public theologians of various nationalities and denominations reveals a fascinating diversity, richness, and frequent overlapping, and at the same time provides interesting insights into the possible origins of public theology, together with its underlying motivational and theological foundations.

The term "public theology" first appeared, according to Max Stackhouse, in the title of a 1974 study of the work of Reinhold Niebuhr (1892–1971) by Martin E. Marty: *Reinhold Niebuhr: Public Theology and the American Experience*. Stackhouse goes on to suggest that it was the natural outcome of Niebuhr's understanding of the role of religion and the nature of the church:

> The term was used to stress the point that theology, while related to intensely personal commitments and to a particular community of worship, is at its most profound level, neither merely private nor a matter of distinctive communal identity. Rather, it is an argument regarding the way things are and ought to be, one decisive for public discourse and necessary to the guidance of individual souls, societies, and indeed, the community of nations.[8]

6. Jacobsen, *Models of Public Theology*, 8.

7. Breitenberg, E. Harold, Jr. "To Tell the Truth, Will the Real Public Theology Please Stand up." *The Journal of the Society of Christian Ethics* 23.2 (Fall/Winter 2003) 70.

8. Stackhouse, Max L. "Public Theology and Ethical Judgement." *Theology Today* (1997). https://journals.sagepub.com/doi/abs/10.1177/004057369705400203.

The Center for Public Theology, on the other hand, espouses the opinion that the term "public theology" derives from Martin Marty's 1981 modification of the term "public religion," originally used in 1749 by Benjamin Franklin. Marty later developed the term in conversation with Robert Bellah's scholarship on "civil religion." He goes on to explain that, while a sociologist can reconstruct a civil religion from historical materials to ground a moral criticism, a public theologian, on the other hand, being closer to experienced religious identities, can challenge citizens in terms of their religious commitment in their respective churches, synagogues, or mosques.

Marty's own definition of the term is clear-cut: "When the public church reflexively examines and critiques existing social practices and cultural understandings in the light of its deepest religious insights into justice and the good society, it does public theology."[9]

According to Scott R. Paeth in *Moltmann, Modernity and Public Theology*, Marty's contemporary, the German Reformed theologian, Jurgen Moltmann, is of the opinion that: "Public theology strives to uncover the theological issues that underlie human culture, society, and experience." He continues: "When Moltmann defines his theology as 'public theology', he specifies that he means by this 'Kingdom of God theology.'"[10] Kingdom-of-God public theology strives to uncover the theological issues that underlie human culture, intervenes critically and prophetically in the public affairs of a given society, and draws public attention, not to the church's own interests, but to God's Kingdom. Public theology, as Moltmann understands it, is not simply a description of the social function of the church in a pluralistic democracy, but a call to action to Christians to take sides and to embody Christ's rule in their lives. It is public because it recognizes the sovereignty of God over every human venue and activity, and knows of no corner of human affairs where God is not active in bringing about his reign. And it

---

9. Marty, Martin. "Public Theology." Center for Public Theology. http://www.pubtheo.com/section.asp?id=1011 (no longer accessible).

10. Paeth, *Exodus, Church and Civil Society*, 232.

is this understanding of the intersection of "public" with "theology" that can give good grounds for an understanding of society and a social ethic that is a true theology of hope. This term is used frequently by Moltmann to emphasize the church's public commitment to a broader understanding of theology's public task, which takes into account the plurality of ends and institutions within society. The idea of the "Exodus Church" enables deeper understanding of Christian ethical participation within a complex modern society. Moltmann argues strenuously for Christian discipleship and public theology that take sides. In both critical and creative ways, he advances the specific relevance of Christian messianic hope to today's thorniest political, economic, and ecological questions—including human rights, environmental rights, globalization, market capitalism, fundamentalisms, and Jewish-Christian relations—and the deeper values contested therein.

The thought of the Catholic theologian, David Tracy, on "public theology" in a pluralistic society has been evolving gradually. Based on his conviction that religion is by no means a private affair, given the "universality of the divine reality,"[11] in 1981 he addressed the necessarily public character of systematic theology in *Analogical Imagination*. Systematic theologians, he posits, need to enter into conversation with and from social reality, or "the public." He goes on to speak of not just one but "three publics" or participants in this conversation with theology: the academy, the church, and the public realm, or wider society, because theologians are members of all three publics—as citizens, as intellectuals, and as believers. Tracy's theologians, therefore, serve God and neighbor, but more specifically through a public conversation about the very questions of meaning and purpose that all people, in some way or another, ask in their everyday lives. Tracy, according to T. Howland Sanks, has become increasingly sensitive of the need to include other voices in the conversation, and widens it to include voices of the poor, of women, of blacks, and of all the marginalized. "It is no small matter," he says, "that there are now many 'others' who do

---

11. Tracy, *Analogical Imagination*, 51.

theology in ways very different, even conflictually other, from my own white, male, middle class, and academic."[12]

Similarly, the Scottish theologian and founder of the Center for Theology and Public Issues at Edinburgh University, Duncan Forrester, hailed as "one of the most influential proponents of public theology," succinctly defined it as a theology which "attends to the Bible and the tradition of faith at the same time as it attempts to discern the signs of the times and understand what is going on in the light of the gospel."[13]

William Storrar, a colleague of Forrester, widens the scope of both the "who" and the "what" of public theology. He describes it as "a collaborative exercise in theological reflection, on public issues which is prompted by disruptive social experiences that call for a thoughtful and faithful response" and motivated by "public anger" and "public spirit." Dr. Storrar includes the stranger and the citizen among those who "do public theology" and "gift us in the global era."[14]

Further afield, but following in the footsteps of Storrar, Andries van Aarde, writing from the University of Pretoria, South Africa, takes an unconventional approach. A professional theologian from the academic world, he argues that public theology is "not about theologians or pastors 'doing theology.'" For van Aarde, it is not about academic papers, lectures, or textbooks. Rather public theology emerges in "movies, songs, poems and novels, art, architecture, protest marches, clothing, newspaper and magazine articles."[15] Its protagonists are poets, writers, and artists. I think of Oprah Winfrey and her relatively new television series, "Belief," or David Baldacci's novel about human trafficking, "The Forgotten," and Jim Wallis's books and blog.

---

12. Tracy, *Dialogue with the Other*, 6.

13. Mannion, "A Brief Genealogy of Public Theology," 123.

14. Storrar, William. "Lecture 1: Public anger: the stranger's gift in a global era." "Lecture 2: Public spirit—the citizen's gift in a global era." At symposium at the University of Pretoria: Doing Public Theology in a Global Era.

15. van Aarde, Andries. "What is "theology" in "public theology" and what is "public" about "public theology"?" *HTS Teologiese Studies* 64.3 (2008) a81.

The What, Why, and How of Public Theology

Walter Bruggeman, a contemporary biblical theologian, renowned for his theological acumen and social awareness, finds his motivation for challenging the status quo in reading Scripture, the Word of God, in contemporary contexts. In an interview with one of the editors of *Theology of Ferguson* he commented:

> Insofar as the ancient prophets protested against injustice, violence, and exploitation (and that rhetoric continues to be pertinent in our context of brutality and exploitation). It is that kind of abrasive speech we cannot easily welcome into settled and stable society but then again, it wasn't welcomed the first time. I think the scriptures are important because they both model that kind of speech and they authorize that kind of speech for our use in our circumstance.

He continues:

> It is in the narratives and the psalms. Beginning with the Exodus narrative and the Elijah narrative and the Jesus narrative, they are all storied about public transformation that happened by courage of uncredentialed people. These kinds of narratives feed our imagination and give us energy and courage.[16]

Again, in *The Alternative World of the Psalms*, Bruggemann confesses that his favorite prophet is Jeremiah. "I always tell my students that Jeremiah certainly reads like it was written yesterday about our crises. But my pietistic tradition sort of taught that the way you live out holiness is by caring for the vulnerable neighbor."[17]

Whereas David Bromell, a New Zealander, in his article, "What is Public Theology?" places the "how" of public theology firmly back on the academic campus, declaring that "Public theology is a form of applied theology. It reflects critically on the ethical and political implications, here and now, of claims expressed or

---

16. Jones, Micky. "Models and Authorizations: An Interview with Walter Bruggemann." https://medium.com/theology-of-ferguson/models-and-authorizations-an-interview-with-walter-bruggemann-3ab5ecd96c20#215.p3yrjdeeq.

17. Brueggemann, Walter. *Alternative World of the Psalms*. Seattle University (2013). http://www.spu.edu./centers/cbte/bruggemann-lecture.asp.

implied in religious faith and witness, and does so in the public sphere, in publicly accessible ways . . . It's critical thinking, with others, about religious faith and public life."[18]

David Hollenbach, SJ, disagreed with the privatization of religion but takes his defense of "public theology" a step further, arguing that "For both theological and political reasons, religious discourse deserves to be a free participant in the public exchange of a pluralistic society."[19] He explains that "the free exercise of religion is a social freedom and the right to freedom of religion includes the right to seek to influence the policies and laws by which a free people will be governed and the public culture they share."[20] Hollenbach devotes the last chapter of his book to a consideration of the public role of religious communities beyond Christianity to other religious traditions, such as Confucianism and Islam and the possibility of a common moral ground in the face of religious pluralism. He makes a vigorous plea for respect for the religious and cultural freedom of the diverse communities in our world, in the context of dialogue in pursuit of an effective global ethic.

Finally, we return again to the Unites States and yet another acclaimed public theologian, Max Stackhouse, who "points towards a wider and deeper strand of theological reflection rooted in the interaction of biblical insight, philosophical analysis, historical discernment and social formation."[21] In *Public Theology for a Global Society*, essays written as a tribute to Stackhouse, several leading Christian scholars consider the historical roots and ongoing resources of public theology as a vital element in the church's engagement with global issues. They explore the concept of public theology and the challenge of relating theological claims to a larger social and political context. They refer to public theology as both

---

18. Bromell, David. "What is Public Theology?" University of Itago (May 2011). http://www.otago.ac.nz/ctpi/otago032508.pdf.

19. Hollenbach, *Global Face of Public Faith*, 118.

20. Hollenbach, *Global Face of Public Faith*, 14.

21. Stackhouse, Max L. "Public Theology." In *The Dictionary of the Ecumenical Movement*, edited by Nicholas Lossky et al. 54, 165. Geneva: World Council of Churches, 2002.

theological practice and public speech, and consider the potential and limits of public theology in ecumenical and international networks.

These definitions of the term "public theology," though varied, do reveal certain common characteristics. In all of them, public theology is about the church in the world and has ecumenical and global dimensions. It is at the same time social, political, and immensely practical. But, above all, in the words of Gerard Mannion: "It is theology concerned with *ethical* questions and challenges,"[22] the questions and challenges posed by international events and the politics in our world today.

It is Mannion's understanding of the "what" of public theology that resonates most for me and I have taken it as a basis for my reflection on the Handmaids of the Sacred Heart's decision to become practitioners of theology in the public square. His thoughts on public theology seem to me to be the closest to those of the Sisters. Like Mannion, the Handmaids view public theology, whether in the academy, the churches or in the world, as a constitutive role of the church, and themselves as members of that church: a church that is oriented *ad extra,* reaching out to our secular and pluralistic society; a church that is defined by *Gaudium et Spes* and that makes its own "the hopes and joys, the griefs and anxieties"[23] of humanity; a church that is concerned with everything that happens in the world, celebrating what is best and resisting the worst. The Handmaids want to espouse the theology that Mannion defines as one that makes a positive difference and that offers a channel for their care and concern for the poor and vulnerable. In this sense, public theology is a way in which they can bring God's compassion and the gospel to the international community. For the Handmaids, it is a theology that is aligned with their foundational mission and identity, and with the Eucharist. It is a theology that heals, reconciles, challenges, and transforms. It is a theology that is essentially active.

---

22. Mannion, "A Brief Genealogy of Public Theology," 122.
23. Vatican Council II, *Gaudium et Spes,* 1.

Turning to the "how" of public theology, it is important to distinguish between the *term* "public theology" and what public theology looks like in practice in the lives and ministry of those who engage in it. Both Mannion and Stackmann are of the opinion that the term "public theology," while relatively new, is preceded by a long history of public theology happening, if not yet named as such. Stackhouse qualifies his initial statement, placing the origin of the term "public theology" in the 1970s, by adding an important rider. He states that the term "appeared as the summary of a long tradition." Similarly, in *A Brief Genealogy of Public Theology, or, Doing Theology when it Seems Nobody is Listening*, Gerard Mannion, after discussing the development in the later twentieth century of explicit "public theology," looks back to key periods of the history of the church where he finds many forms of public theology being "done." In his opinion, there has always been public theology because "this relates, and very much so, to the mission of the church—particularly the understandings of that mission *ad extra*."[24]

To illustrate his point, Mannion takes his readers on a rapid journey through church history beginning with the life and ministry of Jesus Christ, "who spoke in public places and addressed the public and social contexts and leaders of his day,"[25] and the life of the early church. The Acts of the Apostles and the Letters of St. Paul, he suggests, point to a similar engagement, notably St. Paul's speech on the Areopagus. "The earliest Christians in fact went one stage further in adopting the term and concept from public discourse that would give the church its very name—*Ecclesia*."[26]

It is impossible, in this short chapter, to do justice to Mannion's fascinating and all-inclusive sweep through the centuries. In it, he cites innumerable examples of what is essentially public theology happening in all but name, continually and everywhere, each one rising to meet the challenges posed by its own context. Therefore, I will limit myself to singling out those only that are

24. Mannion, "A Brief Genealogy of Public Theology," 122.
25. Mannion, "A Brief Genealogy of Public Theology," 128.
26. Mannion, "A Brief Genealogy of Public Theology," 128.

relevant to my own thought, and in my own context of belonging to a religious order committed to serving the poor.

Mannion emphasizes the contribution of the founders of religious orders to shaping public theology, notably St. Ignatius of Loyola, who "formed the society of Jesus, literally to exercise a profound influence in the wider and societal and public realms."[27] He does not discount the role of women, including Margery Kempe, Julian of Norwich, Catherine of Siena, and Mary Ward who, each in their own way, tried to bring theology to the public square.

In the context of the imperial expansion of Europe that provided a new context for an interplay between theology and a public life, dominated as it was by greed and injustice, Mannion includes Bartolomé de las Casas, who was inspired by Scripture to proclaim the gospel in defense of the native peoples of Latin America, who were oppressed by the conquistadores in a society being established on a foundation of plunder and brutality. His justification was clear: "Christ did not die for gold."[28]

Moving into the nineteenth and twentieth century, Mannion observes that "public theology" was growing all around the globe. He notes the importance of the social gospel, adding that Leo XIII "delved into the concerns and challenges of who we now call public theology through his pontificate."[29] Leo XIII's encyclical *Rerum Novarum*, in response to the social issues resulting from the industrial revolution and the growth of capitalism, is considered the foundational text of modern Catholic social teaching. Mannion also highlights the development of interfaith dimensions.

Mannion concludes his "genealogy" of public theology with the assertion:

> By the 1990's, the fight against the dehumanizing forces of globalization perhaps became the main issue in the realm of public theology. And a new generation of Christian charities and NGOs, which began to emerge in the

---

27. Mannion, "A Brief Genealogy of Public Theology," 131.
28. Gutierrez, *Las Casas*, 420.
29. Mannion, "A Brief Genealogy of Public Theology," 136.

1950s and 1960s were also putting public theology into practice in many different ways.[30]

The "why" of a distinctive public theology can be attributed, in part, to ecclesiological developments and a growing awareness of ethical issues. There has been a shift in the understanding of the church's role in the world: it has widened its horizon to embrace a global worldview, and, in that context, engage in a moral conversation with others rather than setting rules and regulations for its own members. It has recovered its identity as mission-centered, *ad extra*. Religion and spirituality have reached out rather than looked inward in a self-centered focus on personal sanctification. Theologians have discovered the wider public relevance of their work. Believers have recaptured the message of the biblical prophets and of Jesus Christ.

At the same time, issues such as the human rights, the common good, poverty, debt, famine, drought, and emerging bioethical and environmental challenges have become increasingly important in our vocabulary and in our engagement. Social media has heightened our awareness of what is happening in our world and the crises that face us. These issues have challenged the ethical imagination of so many individuals and communities who, each in their own context and with their relevant skills and expertise, want to make the world a better place. This is what Walter Bruggemann calls "The continuing subversion of alternative possibilities."[31] That is what public theology is about. Because, as Forrester says in "Working in the Quarry": "What we need is a theology which makes a difference, a theology that heals, reconciles, helps, challenges. Perhaps we need more theologians who are angry, and determined to make a difference."[32] Public theology is theology that makes a positive difference in society at large.

---

30. Mannion, "A Brief Genealogy of Public Theology," 140.
31. Brueggemann, *Journey to the Common Good*, 37.
32. Quoted in Mannion, "A Brief Genealogy of Public Theology," 152.

Chapter 2

Public Theology and Catholic Social Teaching

IN HIS PAPER ENTITLED "A Brief Genealogy of Public Theology," Gerard Mannion includes the beginnings of Catholic social teaching as one of the many forms of public theology that was "being done" but not yet named and which was part of the long tradition that preceded the use of the term "public theology." In this chapter, I look closely at the ongoing role of Catholic social teaching as a player on the public stage and how it has influenced and has been influenced by public debate on social issues.

Catholic social teaching is the body of doctrine developed by the Catholic Church on matters of social justice. It is essentially based on Scripture which is the Word of a God who hears the cry of the poor and delights in justice. Its roots are in the Hebrew prophets who burned with God's special love for the widow, the orphan, and the immigrant, and who called God's people to a covenant of steadfast love, justice, and righteousness. It is also a teaching founded on the life and words of Jesus Christ, who incarnated God's passion for justice in his mission "to bring good news to the poor" (Luke 4:18–19), and who identified himself with "the least of these," the hungry and the stranger (cf. Matt 25:45). Hence,

Scripture provides a theological foundation for the commitment to the poor and to the justice upon which Catholic social teaching is built.

Modern Catholic social teaching emerged, according to Mannion, "out of the pressing need for a public theology in challenging times."[1] Those "challenging times" referred specifically to the mid- and late-nineteenth century, marked by the transformation and social repercussions in Europe that were brought about by the industrial revolution. It was the contemporary Pope, Leo XIII (b. 1810, Pope from 1878, d. 1903), who, from the beginning of his pontificate, engaged in the social and ethical discussion that we now call public theology. He issued a number of letters on political and social issues, both local and international,[2] prior to the promulgation of his famous encyclical *Rerum Novarum* (On Capital and Labor) in 1891, a landmark document that is the foundational text of modern Catholic social teaching.

Leo XIII began his encyclical with a brief analysis of the social changes caused by the process of industrialization in Europe:

> That the spirit of revolutionary change, which has long been disturbing the nations of the world, should have passed beyond the sphere of politics and made its influence felt in the cognate sphere of practical economics is not surprising. The elements of the conflict now raging are unmistakable, in the vast expansion of industrial pursuits and the marvelous discoveries of science; in the changed relations between masters and workmen; in the enormous fortunes of some few individuals, and the utter poverty of the masses; the increased self-reliance and closer mutual combination of the working classes; as also, finally, in the prevailing moral degeneracy.[3]

Writing from the Catholic Church's newfound understanding of its role in civil society and its mission to contribute to conversation and debate in the public square, Leo continues: "The momentous

---

1. Mannion, "A Brief Genealogy of Public Theology," 163.
2. Notably, *Aeterni Patris* (1879).
3. Leo XIII, *Rerum Novarum*, 1.

Public Theology and Catholic Social Teaching

gravity of the state of things now obtaining fills every mind with painful apprehension; wise men are discussing it; practical men are proposing schemes; popular meetings, legislatures, and rulers of nations are all busied with it—actually there is no question which has taken deeper hold on the public mind."[4]

The Pope goes on to address the results of the excesses of the industrial revolution which he characterizes as: "The misery and wretchedness pressing so unjustly on the majority of the working class."[5] He calls for increased social protection and labor rights for the poor, while emphasizing the relationship between owners and workers, between capital and labor, together with their mutual rights and obligations.

Rerum Novarum was the first text in what was to become a growing corpus of literature and reflection called Catholic social teaching. Since then, until the present day, the Catholic Church has continued to engage in public theology, attempting to respond to contemporary challenges as a consistent critic of social injustice. Successive Popes have added to and developed the Church's social teaching, principally through the medium of encyclical letters, each building on the thought and insights of his predecessors. Conferences of local bishops have also added to the corpus of literature, notably the United States Bishops with their pastoral message entitled *Economic Justice for All*.

At the same time, in an ever-widening context, Catholic social teaching has gradually become more global in its outreach. The "public" it addresses has broadened and become more inclusive. Leo wrote to "Our Venerable Brethren the Patriarchs, Primates, the Archbishops, Bishops, and other ordinaries of places having Peace and Communion with the, Apostolic See."[6] John XXIII added to the list of recipients of papal encyclicals in 1961, "and to the Clergy and Faithful of the entire Catholic World."[7] In 1987, John Paul II included in his readers "all men and women of good

---

4. Leo XIII, *Rerum Novarum*, 1.
5. Leo XIII, *Rerum Novarum*, 3.
6. Leo XIII, *Rerum Novarum*, 1.
7. John XXIII, *Mater and Magistra*, 1.

will"[8] and now, Francis I writes to "every single person who lives on the planet."[9]

The next Pope after Leo XIII to pursue an especially public agenda was Pius XI (b. 1857, Pope from 1922, d. 1939). He did so in the troubling context of the Great Depression, the development of a communist regime in Russia, and the emergence of fascist dictatorships in Germany and Italy. At the very beginning of his pontificate in 1923, he introduced the term "social justice" into the corpus of Catholic teaching in his encyclical, *Studiorum Ducem* (On St. Thomas Aquinas). He later used the term extensively in his social encyclicals, notably in *Quadragesimo Anno* (On Reconstruction of the Social Order) that he penned in 1931 to commemorate the fortieth anniversary of *Rerum Novarum*. "Forty years have passed since Leo XIII's peerless Encyclical, On the Condition of Workers, first saw the light, and the whole Catholic world, filled with grateful recollection, is undertaking to commemorate it with befitting solemnity."[10]

But unlike Leo, who addressed the condition of workers, Pius XI discussed the ethical implications of the social and economic order. He described the major dangers for human freedom and dignity arising from unrestrained capitalism and totalitarian socialism. He also called for the reconstruction of the social order: "Every effort must, therefore, be made that fathers of families receive a sufficient wage adequate to meet ordinary domestic needs. If in the present state of society this is not always feasible, social justice demands that reforms be introduced without delay which will guarantee every adult workingman just such a wage."[11] The new social order, the Pope maintained, should be based on the principle of solidarity and subsidiarity, exemplified by new forms of cooperation and communication between employers and employees. "Government should by its very nature, provide help

---

8. John Paul II, *Sollicitudo Res Socialis* 1.
9. Francis, *Laudato Si*, 1.
10. Pius XI, *Quadragesimo Anno*, 1.
11. Pius XI, *Quadragesimo Anno*, 71.

[*subsidium*] to members of the body social, it should never absorb or destroy them."[12]

A little further on, Pius concludes his argument: "To that end (i.e., that social justice and social charity regulate the economic order), all the institutions of public and social life must be imbued with the spirit of justice, and this justice must, above all, be truly operative. It must build up a juridical and social order able to pervade all economic activity."[13] In 1937, at the height of the Nazi oppression, Pius XI wrote an encyclical in German, *Mit Brennender Sorge* (On the Church and the German Reich), that was secretly smuggled into Germany to be read in all German Catholic Churches on Palm Sunday, the beginning of Passion Week. The encyclical denounced the government of National Socialism in Germany and was published just days before *Divini Redemptoris* (Of the Divine Redeemer), a similar condemnation of communism in Russia. In *Mit Brennender Sorge*, Pius XI criticized National Socialism both for its disproportionate emphasis on the priority of the state and race over and above God and church, and for its discriminatory racial policies.

> Whoever exalts race, or the people, or the State, or a particular form of State, or the depositories of power, or any other fundamental value of the human community—however necessary and honorable be their function in worldly things—whoever raises these notions above their standard value and divinizes them to an idolatrous level, distorts and perverts an order of the world planned and created by God; he is far from the true faith in God and from the concept of life which that faith upholds.[14]

Pius XI, now in failing health, continued to be deeply disturbed by racism and Nazi ideology. So much so that, in 1938, he ordered a *Syllabus Against Racism* be issued and distributed to all Catholic Universities, but died before he could approve and release it.

---

12. Pius XI, *Quadragesimo Anno*, 79.
13. Pius XI, *Quadragesimo Anno*, 88.
14. Pius XI, *Mit Brennender Sorge*, 8.

John XXIII's (b.1881, Pope from 1958, d. 1963) great legacy to the church and the world was reading the "signs of the times," or the main characteristics that were emerging in the latter half of the twentieth century. In his "Opening Speech of Vatican Council II," John stated: "She [the Church] must ever look to the present, to the new conditions and new forms of life introduced into the modern world which have opened new avenues to the Catholic apostolate."[15] He later identified as important "signs of the times": the women's movement, the movement for workers' rights, and the ending of colonialism. This new approach to the world or "historical consciousness", is an awareness that is based on the conviction that God is at work in human history and invites us to interact with the realities that make up that history. His social encyclicals demonstrated just how much the church had learned from and contributed to those realities with regard to human rights.

John XXIII made two major contributions to the corpus of Catholic social teaching: *Mater et Magistra*, (Christianity and Social Progress), 1961, and *Pacem in Terris*, (Peace on Earth), 1963. In both encyclicals, he introduced the idea that "human dignity" is the heart of Catholic social teaching and the foundation of all human rights. In John XXIII's words: "This teaching rests on one basic principle: individual human beings are the foundation, the cause and the end of every social institution. That is necessarily so, for men are by nature social beings. This fact must be recognized, as also the fact that they are raised in the plan of Providence to an order of reality which is above nature". He continues: "On this basic principle, which guarantees the sacred dignity of the individual, the Church constructs her social teaching".[16] *Mater et Magistra*, issued to commemorate the seventieth anniversary of *Rerum Novarum* in 1961, reexamines the social and economic issues originally addressed by Leo XIII but within the post-war milieu. John wanted to reflect on the lessons the Catholic Church

---

15. John XXIII. "Opening Speech of Vatican Council II." https://www.crossroadsinitiative.com/media/articles/opening-speech-to-second-vatican-council/.

16. John XXIII, *Mater et Magistra*, 219–220.

and the world had learned in the years between 1891 and 1961, calling attention to the significant scientific, technological, social, and political changes that had taken place in this new world.[17]

Building on Leo XIII's foundation, and applying the teachings of his predecessors to modern problems, John praised the potential of science and technology for increasing the standard of living, but warned about its potential for restricting human freedom. He argued that economic policies must be balanced so that all classes would benefit from technological advance.

The Pope defended private property as a natural right and encouraged workers to organize in order to secure a just wage. But John XXIII also introduced new issues and concerns into the corpus of Catholic social teaching. A new focus was the special attention he dedicated to the plight of the farmers and farm workers in depressed agricultural economies:

> Nearly every country, therefore, is faced with this fundamental problem: What can be done to reduce the disproportion in productive efficiency between agriculture on the one hand, and industry and services on the other; and to ensure that agricultural living standards approximate as closely as possible those enjoyed by city dwellers, who draw their resources either from industry or from the services in which they are engaged? What can be done to persuade agricultural workers that, far from being inferior to other people, they have every opportunity of developing their personality through their work, and can look forward to the future with confidence?[18]

The Pope also focused on the reality of the many new nations emerging from the grip of the western colonial powers and outlined a human rights-based international relations framework. He wrote, "Probably the most difficult problem today concerns the relationship between political communities that are economically advanced and those in the process of development. Whereas the standard of living is high in the former, the latter are subject to

17. John XXIII, *Mater et Magistra*, 47–49.
18. John XXIII, *Mater et Magistra*, 125.

extreme poverty."[19] John XXIII went on to denounce the growing economic disparity both between and within nations, and challenged wealthy nations to share their resources with the newly independent nations without infringing upon their autonomy or their right to political self-determination.[20] Finally, John XXIII prioritized the importance of the common good. He urged governments to enact national policies that would advance the common good.[21]

But the justification of all government action is the common good. Public authority, therefore, must bear in mind the interests of the state as a whole; which means that it must promote all three areas of production—agriculture, industry, and services—simultaneously and evenly. Everything must be done to ensure that citizens of the less developed areas are treated as responsible human beings, and are allowed to play a major role in achieving their own economic, social and cultural advancement.

John XXIII widened the scope of the common good to embrace the whole international community, calling for a greater awareness of the need for all peoples to live as one community with a common good. "To this end, a sane view of the common good must be present and operative in men invested with public authority. They must take account of all those social conditions which favor the full development of human personality."[22]

In *Pacem in Terris*, John XXIII went even further. Drafted two months before the Pope died in 1963, in the middle of the Cold War, two years after the erection of the Berlin Wall, and just months after the Cuban Missile Crisis—during which the Vatican had served as an intermediary between the White House and the Kremlin—the encyclical addressed the problem of world peace and in particular nuclear non-proliferation. *Pacem in Terris* has been described as "an event" rather than a papal document. It was a public theology event that captured the imagination of a global

19. John XXIII, *Mater et Magistra*, 157.
20. John XXIII, *Mater et Magistra*, 157–165.
21. John XXIII, *Mater et Magistra*, 151.
22. John XXIII, *Mater et Magistra*, 65.

audience, not just Catholics but also caring men and women well beyond Catholic circles. Its impact was due both to its timing, its context, and its message. It was the first papal encyclical to be published verbatim in the *New York Times*, while *The Washington Post* reported, "*Pacem in Terris* is not just the voice of an old priest, nor just that of an ancient Church; it is the voice of the conscience of the world." This was the very first encyclical that a Pope addressed to "all men of good will," not just to Catholics. According to Mary Ann Glendon: "He was insisting that the responsibility for setting conditions for peace does not just belong to the great and powerful of the world—it belongs to each and every one of us."[23]

Added to John's inclusive responsibility, were his prophetic warnings against all war in a nuclear age and against nuclear proliferation in particular, and his passionate recommendation that conflicts "should not be resolved by recourse to arms, but rather by negotiation."[24]

But *Pacem in Terris* radically affected Catholic social teaching not only on war and peace, but also on church-state relations, womens' rights, including the rightful equality of women in public life, religious freedom, international relations, and other major issues. The core of the encyclical was Pope John's analysis of the intrinsic dignity of every human person—with its implications for human rights, religious freedom, concern for the poor, rights of developing nations, possibilities of stronger international institutions to address the then-incipient issues of globalization, and other key social and political concerns.

> Any well-regulated and productive association of men in society demands the acceptance of one fundamental principle: that each individual man is truly a person. His is a nature, that is, endowed with intelligence and free will. As such he has rights and duties, which together flow as a direct consequence from his nature. These rights and duties are universal and inviolable, and therefore altogether inalienable.[25]

23. Catholic World Report, June 14, 2013.
24. John XXIII, *Pacem in Terris*, 126.
25. John XXIII, *Pacem in Terris*, 9.

He continues:

> When, furthermore, we consider man's personal dignity from the standpoint of divine revelation, inevitably our estimate of it is incomparably increased. Men have been ransomed by the blood of Jesus Christ. Grace has made them sons and friends of God, and heirs to eternal glory.[26]

Arguing from both natural law and revelation, John XXIII proposed ethical standards not just for Christians, but for all peoples and all cultures, and the promotion of the common good in a religiously pluralistic world. The Pope went on to propose a charter of universal human rights very similar to those contained in the United Nations Universal Declaration. He affirmed that the protection of human rights was the basis for world peace:

> But first we must speak of man's rights. Man has the right to live. He has the right to bodily integrity and to the means necessary for the proper development of life, particularly food, clothing, shelter, medical care, rest, and, finally, the necessary social services. In consequence, he has the right to be looked after in the event of ill health, disability stemming from his work, widowhood, old age, enforced unemployment, or whenever through no fault of his own he is deprived of the means of livelihood.[27]

But John XXIII also "triggered what was to prove a momentous watershed in the Roman Catholic Church. It was he who set in motion that sea change which transformed the Church from a static, authoritarian Church that spoke in monologues, to a dynamic, sisterly Church hat promoted dialogue."[28] The Pope pulled that trigger when he convened the Second Vatican Council. John's aim was to bring about *aggiornamento* in the Catholic Church and,

---

26. John XXIII, *Pacem in Terris*, 10.

27. John XXIII, *Pacem in Terris*, 11.

28. Konig, Franz. "It Must Be the Holy Spirit." *The Tablet* (December 21, 2002). https://www.bc.edu/content/dam/files/research_sites/cjl/texts/cjrelations/resiurces/articles/konig.htm.

in so doing, he radically changed the relationship of the Catholic Church with the whole world.

John XXIII's inductive approach, based on reading the signs of the times, had a significant influence on Vatican II, which began in October 1962 and, after John XXIII's death, continued through 1965 under the pontificate of Paul VI (b. 1897, Pope from 1963, d. 1978).

"The Church should never depart from the sacred treasure of truth inherited from the Fathers. But at the same time, she must ever look to the present, to the new conditions and the new forms of life introduced into the modern world."[29] This approach, together with the commitment to dialogue, introduced by John XXIII and further underscored by Paul VI, confirmed the role of the Catholic Church as a very active and vocal protagonist of public theology.

Vatican II was an assembly of Catholic bishops drawn from all over the world, from diverse cultures and from countries where all the world's great religions played significant roles. It was the first time that the Catholic Church officially presented herself as a world church rather than as a European religion to be exported to the rest of the world along with European culture. This provided the groundwork for a public theological declaration of common ground and values in a world of cultural and religious pluralism and broadened the Church's outreach to include inter-Christian ecumenical dialogue and dialogue with the other great world religions. In *Nostra Aetate*, (Declaration on the Relation of the Church with Non-Christian Religions), 1965, the Council Fathers exhorted Christians and Muslims to "preserve as well as to promote together for the benefit of all mankind social justice and moral welfare, as well as peace and freedom."[30]

Gaudium et Spes (Pastoral Constitution of the Church in the Modern World), one of the last documents to be promulgated by Vatican II and, easily, the most groundbreaking of all them, was not planned for at the outset of the council—rather it came

29. John XXIII, *Opening Statement Vatican II*.
30. Vatican II, *Nostra Aetate*, 3.

as a complete surprise. Towards the end of the first session of the council, the Belgian Cardinal Suenens pointed out that instead of concentrating on internal church matters, the council should turn its attention to the world and embrace it. The result was *Gaudium et Spes* that emphasized the intimate connection between faith and social responsibility and thrust the Catholic Church more deeply into interaction with the world:

> The joys and the hopes, the griefs and the anxieties of the men of this age, especially those who are poor or in any way afflicted, these are the joys and hopes, the griefs and anxieties of the followers of Christ. Indeed, nothing genuinely human fails to raise an echo in their hearts. For theirs is a community composed of men. United in Christ, they are led by the Holy Spirit in their journey to the Kingdom of their Father and they have welcomed the news of salvation which is meant for every man. That is why this community realizes that it is truly linked with mankind and its history by the deepest of bonds.[31]

"This conciliar text," according to David Hollenbach writing in *America Magazine,*

> laid out the most challenging vision of the church's social mission of the modern era. It proclaimed that the Catholic community should be deeply engaged in promoting the dignity of every person . . . It taught that Christian faith reveals the deeper meaning of this-worldly activity, calling believers to transform the workplace and the civic forum into more authentic reflections of the communion God wants all people to share in the heavenly city.[32]

Hollenbach claims that this text had a lasting impact and bore significant fruit later in the church's participation in the struggle for human rights in Chile, Poland, El Salvador, Korea, the Philippines, and elsewhere. It challenged the church to help forge new bonds of global solidarity, mobilizing the church to lead the Jubilee

---

31. Vatican II, *Gaudium et Spes*, 1.

32. Hollenbach, David. "Joy and Hope, Grief and Anguish." *America Magazine* (December 5, 2005).

2000 campaign to alleviate the debt of the poorest countries and to become one of the world's strongest advocates of multilateral approaches in international politics.

Finally, the very last text approved by the council, *Dignitatis Humanae* (Declaration on Religious Freedom*)*, brought about a dramatic change in the Catholic Church's position on religious liberty by asserting religious freedom for all, based on the dignity of the human person and the limits of democratic government. (The earlier position denied religious liberty on the basis that error has no rights.) It also rejected implicitly "the outmoded notion that 'religion is a purely private affair' or that the 'Church belongs to the sacristy'. Religion is relevant to the life and action of society. Therefore, religious freedom includes the right to point out this societal relevance of religious belief."[33] After Vatican II, Paul VI's task was to implement the council's mandates and, in doing so, he repeatedly "pointed out its societal relevance." The pontiff had much to say on social justice issues and was a major contributor to the development of Catholic social teaching. He was the first Pope to address the United Nations; in 1965, in the context of the escalating war in Vietnam, armed conflicts being waged in many countries and Cold War tensions, he pleaded for peace.

> There is no need for a long talk to proclaim the main purpose of your Institution. It is enough to recall that the blood of millions, countless unheard-of sufferings, useless massacres and frightening ruins have sanctioned the agreement that unites you with an oath that ought to change the future history of the world: never again war, never again war! It is peace, peace, that has to guide the destiny of the nations of all mankind![34]

Nicknamed "the Pilgrim Pope," Paul VI was also the first Pope to travel the world, visiting all of six continents. He went to the Holy Land in 1964 and attended eucharistic congresses both in

---

33. Heyer, *Prophetic and Public*, 33.

34. Paul VI, "Address to United Nations," (1965). http://w2.vatican.va/content/paul-vi/en/speeches/1965/documents/hf_p-vi_spe_19651004_united-nations.html.

Bombay, (now Mumbai) India and, later, in Bogota, Colombia. Denied permission to visit Poland in 1966, Paul ventured on to Portugal, Turkey, Switzerland, Uganda, West Asia, Oceania, and Australia. With his journeys, Paul VI opened many new avenues for the papacy and also public theology forums by "speaking out, though diplomatically, on every conceivable topic."[35]

In addition, the Pope's travels gave him opportunities to see examples of social injustice with his own eyes, giving him firsthand experience of the sufferings of the poor and oppressed. Paul VI made two major prophetic contributions to the tradition of Catholic social teaching, a 1967 encyclical, *Populorum Progressio* (On the Development of Peoples) and a 1971 apostolic letter, *Octogesima Adveniens* (A Call to Action). In his day, when great economic inequality existed and the rich continued to get richer and the poor continued to get poorer, Paul VI directly challenged this grave injustice. He wrote, "God intended the earth and everything in it for the use of all human beings and peoples. Thus, under the leadership of justice and in the company of charity, created goods should flow fairly to all." He went on to say: "Extreme disparity between nations in economic, social and educational levels provokes jealousy and discord, often putting peace in jeopardy." He continued:

> When we fight poverty, and oppose the unfair conditions of the present, we are not just promoting human wellbeing; we are also furthering man's spiritual and moral development, and hence we are benefiting the whole human race. For peace is not simply the absence of warfare, based on a precarious balance of power; it is fashioned by efforts directed day after day toward the establishment of the ordered universe willed by God, with a more perfect form of justice among men.[36]

Paul VI was also prophetic. Over 40 years ago, he foresaw the impending environmental disaster that is facing humanity today.

---

35. Hebblethwaite, Peter. "Latest Encyclical Seen As Update." *National Catholic Reporter* 26 (February 1988).

36. Paul VI, *Populorum Progressio*, 76.

In his apostolic letter *Octogesima Adveniens*, he warned: "Man is suddenly becoming aware that by an ill-considered exploitation of nature he risks destroying it and becoming in his turn the victim of this degradation."[37]

Paul VI's successor, John Paul II (b.1920, Pope from 1978, d. 2005), contributed three major social encyclicals to the corpus of Catholic social teaching: *Laborem Exercens* (Human Work) in 1981, *Sollicitudo Rei Socialis* (Social Concern) in 1987, and *Centesimus Annus* (100th anniversary of *Rerum Novarum*) in 1991. According to John L. Allen Jr., John Paul II was "a magnificent Pope who presided over a controversial pontificate."[38] John Paul II had a powerful and magnetic personality. He traveled constantly, visiting 130 countries, and was a prolific writer, authoring some 50 major documents and several books. He also produced compact discs and staged massive youth rallies to promote the message of Christ. On the political world stage, John Paul II was a powerful and influential leader who "changed the course of history and helped bring an end to the cold war though his support of Solidarity and the Polish freedom movement. This started the landslide that wiped out Communism in Eastern Europe and, eventually, the Soviet Union."[39]

John Paul II brought to his social teaching the perspective of a moral philosopher, rather than a theologian. At the same time, he also had the personal experience of living under oppressive regimes both as a student in Nazi-occupied Poland, and later as a Catholic pastor in a communist state. With this powerful personal motivation, together with the groundwork laid by his predecessors in bringing faith and theology into the public sphere, "John Paul

---

37. Paul VI, *Octogesima Adveniens*, 21.

38. Allen, John L., Jr. "Obituary of Pope John Paul II." *National Catholic Reporter* (April 2004). http://www.nationalcatholicreporter.org/update/conclave/jp_obit_main.htm.

39. "The Legacy of John Paul II." *America Magazine* (April 18, 2005). https://www.americamagazine.org/faith/2005/04/18/legacy-john-paul-ii.

II," according to Mannion, "could not avoid speaking out on public issues."[40]

John Paul II's passionate belief in the dignity of the human person[41] permeated his teaching on social matters, giving it a distinctive tone. He begins the first of his social encyclicals, *Laborem Exercens*: "I wish to devote this document to human work and, even more, to man in the vast context of the reality of work."[42] In this encyclical, the Pope set out an original scriptural theology of work, based on the first chapter of Genesis. Like previous encyclicals, *Laborem Exercens* is a response to certain social problems of its time, such as automation, rising energy costs, and depletion of natural resources. But for John Paul II, social issues were essentially religious issues. Hence, *Laborem Exercens* provides a reflection on work, beginning with a correct understanding of the human person derived from Scripture. Work, for John Paul, is a fundamental dimension of the human person, called to participate in God's own creative activity by productive labor.

> When man, who had been created "in the image of God . . . male and female", hears the words: "Be fruitful and *multiply, and fill the earth and subdue* it", even though these words do not refer directly and explicitly to work, beyond any doubt they indirectly indicate it as an activity for man to carry out in the world. Indeed, they show its very deepest essence. Man is the image of God partly through the mandate received from his Creator to subdue, to dominate, the earth. In carrying out this mandate, man, every human being, reflects the very action of the Creator of the universe.[43]

Accordingly, the Pope insisted on the principle of the priority of labor over capital and rejected the approach of "considering labor solely according to its economic purpose."[44] Workers, he main-

---

40. Mannion, "A Brief Genealogy of Public Theology," 139.
41. John Paul II, *Laborem Exercens*, 1.
42. John Paul II, *Laborem Exercens*, 1.3.
43. John Paul II, *Laborem Exercens*, 4.
44. John Paul II, *Laborem Exercens*, 13.3.

tained, "are persons, and are therefore, of more value than their products. Through their work, they should be able to transform nature, transforming it into a more fitting habitation for humanity, and at the same time, perfect themselves as persons."[45] After highlighting that the human rights derived from work are, basically, the fundamental rights of the human person, the Pope concludes his thoughts with a restating of the spirituality of work.

Pope John Paul II's encyclical on economic development, *Sollicitudo Rei Socialis*, promulgated on December 30, 1987, came twenty years after *Populorum Progressio*. It updated the Catholic Church's teaching on international development in the light of the changes that had taken place in those two decades, emphasizing its ethical dimensions. After surveying the difficult state of the poor countries, the Pope lays strong blame on the confrontation between the two global blocs: the liberal capitalism of the West, and the Marxist socialism of the East.

> For as we know the tension between East and West is not in itself an opposition between two different levels of development but rather between two concepts of the development of individuals and peoples both concepts being imperfect and in need of radical correction. This opposition is transferred to the developing countries themselves, and thus helps to widen the gap already existing on the economic level between North and South and which results from the distance between the two worlds: the more developed one and the less developed one.[46]

Importantly, in this context, John Paul also introduced two new terms into the vocabulary of social teaching. He refers to the obstacles hindering development as the "structures of sin": "'Sin' and 'structures of sin' are categories which are seldom applied to the situation of the contemporary world. However, one cannot easily gain a profound understanding of the reality that confronts us

---

45. John Paul II, *Laborem Exercens*, 27.
46. John Paul II, *Sollicitudo Rei Socialis*, 21.

unless we give a name to the root of the evils which afflict us."[47] The Pope also calls for a conversion toward solidarity and a "preferential option for the poor," which he designates as a guideline for the church's social doctrine.

> Today, furthermore, given the worldwide dimension which the social question has assumed, this love of preference for the poor, and the decisions which it inspires in us, cannot but embrace the immense multitudes of the hungry, the needy, the homeless, those without medical care and, above all, those without hope of a better future. It is impossible not to take account of the existence of these realities. To ignore them would mean becoming like the "rich man" who pretended not to know the beggar Lazarus lying at his gate.[48]

Importantly also, John Paul II cited the United Nation's promulgation of the Declaration of Human Rights in his encyclical, as an example of progress in the area of awareness of the dignity of the human person.

> At this level one must acknowledge the influence exercised by the Declaration of Human Rights, promulgated some forty years ago, by the United Nations Organization. Its very existence and gradual acceptance by the international community are signs of a growing awareness. The same is to be said, still in the field of human rights, of other juridical instruments issued by the United Nations Organization or other international organizations.[49]

Commenting on Christian social ethics after the Cold War, Hollenbach states: "The dramatic revolutions in Central Europe in 1989 and the collapse of the Soviet Union have had profound effects on Christian social ethical reflection."[50] This is evident in John Paul II's third social encyclical, *Centesimus Annus*, written in 1991 during the last days of the Cold War and the overthrow

---

47. John Paul II, *Sollicitudo Rei Socialis*, 36.
48. John Paul II, *Sollicitudo Rei Socialis*, 42.
49. John Paul II, *Sollicitudo Rei Socialis*, 26.
50. Hollenbach, *Global Face of Public Ethics*, 192.

of communism in his native Poland and other Eastern European countries. In it, the Pope addressed the impact of those upheavals on Catholic social teaching. A very lengthy and complex document, it is partially a refutation of Marxist ideology together with the Pope's explanation of the failure of the socialist economic system. "Socialism," the Pope wrote, "considers the individual person simply as an element, a molecule within the social organism, so that the good of the individual is completely subordinated to the functioning of the socio-economic mechanism."[51] The encyclical, surprisingly, includes the fullest, and in many ways the most positive, treatment of the market economy in any papal document. "It would appear that on the level of individual nations and of international relations, the free market is the most efficient instrument for utilizing resources and effectively responding to needs."[52] "But," he added immediately, "there are many human needs which find no place on the market." But he is convinced that the energies unleashed by the market need to be contained within a "strong juridical framework" and an "ethical and religious" understanding of human freedom, so that the economy is kept in service to the common good.[53]

Besides dealing with economic issues, *Centesimus Annus* also stresses the need for the world to find an alternative to war for resolving disputes. The Pope refers to his repeated appeals against military action in the Persian Gulf:

> I myself, on the occasion of the recent tragic war in the Persian Gulf, repeated my cry: 'Never again war! No, never again war, which destroys the lives of innocent people, teaches how to kill, throws into upheaval even the lives of those who do the killing and leaves behind a trail of resentment and hatred, thus making it all the more difficult to find a solution of the very problems which provoked the war . . . It must never be forgotten that at the root of war there are usually real and serious

51. John Paul II *Centesimus Annus*, 13.
52. John Paul II, *Centesimus Annus*, 34.
53. John Paul II, *Centesimus Annus*, 42.

grievances: injustices suffered, legitimate aspirations frustrated, poverty and the exploitation of multitudes of desperate people who see no real possibility of improving their lot by peaceful means.[54]

John Paul urges imitation of the nonviolent protests in Eastern Europe that brought down a Communist order that many had believed "could only be overturned by another war." "Instead it has been overcome by the non-violent commitment of people who, while always refusing to yield to the force of power, succeeded time after time in finding effective ways of bearing witness to the truth..."[55]

Although his is a persistent voice on behalf of nonviolent solutions to injustice, John Paul also called for "humanitarian intervention" or peacekeeping in trouble spots like Bosnia, Central Africa, and East Timor, even if that meant using force to disarm the aggressor. His advocacy of humanitarian intervention, as much as his praise for nonviolence, contributed to a rethinking of Catholic positions on the use of force in world affairs. Similarly, the Pope's World Day of Peace Message of 2002 allowed for a nation's right to defend itself against global terrorism. However, the right to defense is not the heart of his message, which must be read in a broader context of his teaching on international affairs.

If John Paul II was a philosopher, Benedict XVI (b. 1927, Pope from 2005, resigned 2013) was definitely a systematic theologian. Although Pope Benedict mentioned social justice frequently, he issued his first and only social encyclical *Caritas in Veritate* (Charity in Truth) in July, 2009. Placing his own social teaching in line with Paul VI's *Populorum Progressio* and John Paul II's *Sollicitudo Rei Socialis*, he covered a wide range of issues, including globalization, the financial crisis, labor, technology, and the environment. But Benedict's own teaching on "gratuity and communion" offered a new and radical rethinking on the ethical dimension of economics. He began the encyclical's third chapter by stating that "Charity in truth places man before the astonishing experience of

---

54. John Paul II, *Centesimus Annus*, 52.
55. John Paul II, *Centesimus Annus*, 23.

gift. Gratuitousness is present in our lives in many different forms, which often go unrecognized because of a purely consumerist and utilitarian view of life."[56] "It is from within this understanding," comments David M. Laville, "that Benedict states that economic, social and political development, if it is to be authentically human, needs to make room for the principle of gratuitousness as an expression of fraternity. The extension of gratuity to the market has the goal of making economic exchange more human."[57] Underpinning the whole encyclical is Benedict's conviction that: "Love—caritas—is an extraordinary force which leads people to opt for courageous and generous engagement in the field of justice and peace . . . Charity is at the heart of the church's social doctrine."[58]

Both John Paul II and Benedict XVI were committed to the Catholic Church's social justice teachings. But, according to Michael Sean Winters, writing in the *National Catholic Reporter*,

> Pope Francis has placed those teachings front and center. If the Church's commitment to the poor, its historic and well-founded suspicions of modern consumer capitalism, and its moral horror at the gross income inequality that plagues our planet and each of the societies within that planet, were embraced by previous Popes, they have been made the leitmotif of this first pontiff from the global south.[59]

Pope Francis (b. 1936, Pope from 2013) has contributed, to date, two documents to the corpus of Catholic social teaching: an apostolic exhortation, *Gaudium Evangelii*, (The Joy of the Gospel) in 2013 and an encyclical, *Laudato Si* (Praised Be You) in 2015. His teaching on social issues picks up where his predecessors left

56. Benedict XVI, *Caritas in Veritate*, 34.

57. Laville, David M. *Build Upon Sand: Principle of Gratuity in Pope Benedict XVI's encyclical Caritas in Veritate*. Thesis Toronto School of Theology, 2012. https://tspace.library.utoronto.ca/bitstream/1807/348843/1/Laville_David_201211_MA_thesis.pdf.

58. Benedict XVI, *Caritas in Veritate*, 2.

59. Winters, Michael Sean. "Pope Francis' First Year." *National Catholic Reporter* (March 5, 2014). https://www.ncronline.org/blogs/distinctly-catholic/Pope-francis-first-year-reaction.

off, but in a new and vigorous manner that derives from his pastoral experience and deep spirituality, a manner that is at times very blunt but refreshingly easy to understand! The Pope himself wanted to make very clear that his social teaching is fully integrated into the church's tradition of Catholic social teaching. "It is my hope that this Encyclical Letter, *which is now added to the body of the Church's social teaching*, can help us to acknowledge the appeal, immensity and urgency of the challenge we face."[60]

In *Gaudium Evangelii*, Pope Francis offers a vision of the Catholic Church, summoned by her founder to a "revolution of tenderness"[61] in the context of a "globalization of indifference" and to joyfully announce the Gospel, focusing on the poorest and most vulnerable members of society. Inspired by Jesus's poverty and his care for the deprived and oppressed, Francis writes:

> I want a Church which is poor and for the poor. They have much to teach us. Not only do they share in the *sensus fidei*, but in their difficulties, they know the suffering Christ. We need to let ourselves be evangelized by them. The new evangelization is an invitation to acknowledge the saving power at work in their lives and to put them at the centre of the Church's pilgrim way. We are called to find Christ in them, to lend our voice to their causes, but also to be their friends, to listen to them, to speak for them and to embrace the mysterious wisdom which God wishes to share with us through them.[62]

The Pope continues bluntly, and without hesitation:

> Since this Exhortation is addressed to members of the Catholic Church, I want to say, with regret, that the worst discrimination which the poor suffer is the lack of spiritual care. The great majority of the poor have a special openness to the faith; they need God and we must not fail to offer them his friendship, his blessing, his word, the celebration of the sacraments and a journey of

---

60. Francis, *Laudato Si*, 15.
61. Francis, *Gaudium Evangelii*, 88.
62. Francis, *Gaudium Evangelii*, 198.

growth and maturity in the faith. Our preferential option for the poor must mainly translate into a privileged and preferential religious care.[63]

Francis presses passionately on:

> In this context, we can understand Jesus' command to his disciples: "You yourselves give them something to eat!" (Mk 6:37): it means working to eliminate the structural causes of poverty and to promote the integral development of the poor, as well as small daily acts of solidarity in meeting the real needs which we encounter". And that, continues the Pope, requires "something more than a few sporadic acts of generosity. It presumes the creation of a new mindset which thinks in terms of community and the priority of the life of all over the appropriation of goods by a few.[64]

Pope Francis spells out that new mind set in detail in *Laudato Si.* "Pope Francis' encyclical," comments Jeffrey Sachs,

> is a great and timely gift to humanity. To avoid a catastrophic collision of the world economy and environment, humanity urgently needs to change the trajectory and functioning of the world economy. Yet the world economic system is a juggernaut nearly impervious to coordinated changes at the global scale. *Laudato Si* opens the path to a veritable revolution of ideas to bring about the needed changes.[65]

The encyclical, subtitled *The Care of our Common Home*, begins with a lyrical but passionate description of the climate crisis facing us:

> *LAUDATO SI', mi' Signore*"—"Praise be to you, my Lord". In the words of this beautiful canticle, Saint Francis of Assisi reminds us that our common home is like a sister with whom we share our life and a beautiful

---

63. Francis, *Gaudium Evangelii*, 200.
64. Francis, *Gaudium Evangelii*, 188.
65. Sachs, Jeffrey D. "The Great Gift of Laudato Si." America Magazine (July 6, 2015).

> mother who opens her arms to embrace us.... This sister now cries out to us because of the harm we have inflicted on her by our irresponsible use and abuse of the goods with which God has endowed her. We have come to see ourselves as her lords and masters, entitled to plunder her at will. The violence present in our hearts, wounded by sin, is also reflected in the symptoms of sickness evident in the soil, in the water, in the air and in all forms of life. This is why the earth herself, burdened and laid waste, is among the most abandoned and maltreated of our poor; she "groans in travail" (Rom 8:22).[66]

In *Laudato Si,* Francis lays out a fully integrated theology of the environment which recognizes the fundamental interconnectedness of the economy, society, and environment:

> Today, however, we have to realize that a true ecological approach always becomes a social approach; it must integrate questions of justice in debates on the environment, so as to hear both the cry of the earth and the cry of the poor.[67]

He goes on to say:

> We are faced not with two separate crises, one environmental and the other social, but rather with one complex crisis which is both social and environmental. Strategies for a solution demand an integrated approach to combating poverty, restoring dignity to the excluded, and at the same time protecting nature.[68]

For Francis, the men, women, and children who people the earth are inseparable from the earth.

Laudato Si offers a compelling call to the whole of humanity to conversion and action to create a world in which the economy is, once again, bound by the common good, and in which the common good embraces the reverence for the physical earth and other

---

66. Francis, *Laudato Si,* 1–2.
67. Francis, *Laudato Si,* 49.
68. Francis, *Laudato Si,* 139.

species, creating a new economic system that harnesses technologies and morality to save the planet.

With *Laudato Si,* Pope Francis decisively and controversially entered the public debate on climate change. But Francis's public theology, as that of his predecessors, is by no means limited to papal encyclicals. Francis has a global pulpit which he mounts frequently, be it the balcony of St. Peter's, the audience hall in the Vatican, the podium at the United Nations, the dais at the United States Congress, the aisle of an aircraft, or wherever his pastoral ministry takes him. All echo with Francis's frequent references to caring for the poor and the planet, his trenchant remarks about "savage capitalism," and his calls for government intervention to pursue the common good in the face of hostile market forces. His public statements take many forms: homilies and weekly Angelus messages, impromptu press conferences, off-the-cuff remarks, tweets, videos, and formal speeches to international diplomatic corps.

Francis's actions are, at times, even more eloquent than his words, such as his blank refusal to live in the palatial papal apartments in the Vatican, his provision of showers for the homeless in St. Peter's Square and his visit to a soup kitchen run at the Vatican by the Missionaries of Charity. His most important "stop" in New York City was at Our Lady Queen of Angels School in East Harlem, and on Holy Thursday 2016, he washed the feet of immigrant refugees of different religious faiths. Together with Francis's earlier visit to Lampedusa to mourn the immigrants who died at sea, this was a gesture seen as a powerful public statement, against the background of the spiraling immigrant crisis and growing rejection of Syrian refugees in Europe. Yet another highly charged political statement was Francis's visit to the US-Mexican border in 2016, as was his silent prayer before a dividing wall erected to separate Israel from Palestine in the Holy Land. He is true to his conviction that "A good Catholic meddles in politics."[69] Francis played a key role in opening new diplomatic ties between the United States and

---

69. Francis's homily on September 16, 2013.

Cuba, met with the president of Iran to give a boost to an historic nuclear deal, and weighed in on US airstrikes in Iraq.

To sum up, Catholic social teaching then, as a vehicle of public theology, has responded to the distinctive challenges in politics, economics, and international relations of its context. The first challenge, the industrial revolution and the complex economic changes it brought, was the focus of the encyclicals of Pope Leo XIII and Pius XI. They concentrated on a just wage, subsidiarity, and social justice: all issues that shaped the later social tradition. The second challenge was the internationalization of politics, economics, and war, beginning with World War II and continuing through the Cold War. Catholic social teaching addressed all three topics. The theme of much of the papal teaching of John XXIII, Paul VI and John Paul II, was that the emergence of a truly global international system required a moral vision and a political-legal order that could address changing patterns of governance, the emergence of international institutions, and new security threats in the nuclear age.

John Paul II's *Centesimus Annus,* written after the end of the Cold War and in the midst of the realities of a post-industrial society, marks the third stage of the development of Catholic social teaching. It can be read as the first of the social encyclicals moving towards a new century and a different world order. It underlines the emerging fact of globalization and recognizes the conditions of continuing dehumanizing poverty and, at the same time, societies of great abundance.

In an increasingly complex new world order, characterized by contradictory dynamics of both integration and fragmentation, together with heart-wrenching suffering, Pope Francis represents a unique stage of both continuity and discontinuity in Catholic social teaching. According to Mark Impagliazzo, Francis brings "a new age of political audacity for the Holy See."[70] This "new age"

---

70. Mark Impagliazzo quoted by the *Huffington Post* in "Pope Francis' influence in world politics has made Vatican globally relevant again" (June 4, 2014). https://www.huffingtonpost.com/2014/06/04/Pope-francis-world-politics_n_5448134.html.

is permeated with Francis's personal passion and caring conviction that the Church's social teaching is multifaceted, made up of words, both written and spoken, together with actions and gestures. His public theology is an expression of what he calls a "culture of encounter."[71]

---

71. Allen, John L., Jr. "Francis and the 'Culture of Encounter.'" *National Catholic Reporter* (December 20th, 2013). https://www.ncronline.org/blogs/ncr-today/francis-and-culture-encounter.

Chapter 3

The History, the Mandate, and the Working of the United Nations

THE UNITED NATIONS IS a highly complex organization that was founded in 1945. Since then, its record has been uneven, as its detractors hasten to point out, even though the responsibility for many of its shortcoming lies with its members, while the credit for its successes belong to the institution and its mandate to ensure global peace and security. But it remains today the most important multilateral forum in global politics, as it presides over an ever-expanding agenda that poses unrelenting demands on its time and resources. "The history of the United Nations," according to Stanley Meisler, "bristles with excitement," while the story of the UN as an institution, has "lurched up and down since its beginnings, like a well-plotted movie."[1]

The United Nations Organization was conceived during World War II and, after a long and difficult gestation, was finally born in 1945. Its natural "parents" were the USA and the UK, with sporadic and, at times, contentious input from Russia and China. Its elder brother, the League of Nations was, to all intents and purposes, stillborn, or at least suffered an early demise. Not wishing to

---

1. Meisler, *United Nations*, 3.

witness a second similar tragedy, all the players exhibited extreme caution in the process of bringing the United Nations safely to its full-term birth.

On January 1, 1942, while World War II still raged, Prime Minister Churchill and President Roosevelt, together with the leaders of 24 other states including several "governments in exile," issued a "Declaration by United Nations" committing all the signatories to defeating Adolf Hitler and his allies. Their stated conviction read:

> that complete victory over their enemies is essential to defend life, liberty, independence and religious freedom, and to preserve human rights and justice in their own lands, as well as in other lands, and that they are now engaged in a common struggle against savage and brutal forces seeking to subjugate the world.[2]

Later, other nations gradually joined the coalition, including France in 1944.

Simultaneously, again amidst the complexity and hostilities of war, this political-military alliance was already looking to the future. The priority was, after two devastating world wars and the advent of the nuclear age, to ensure international peace and security for generations to come. But it also began to shape the post-war world with its political, social, and economic challenges by laying the foundations of the organizational structures of what was to become the United Nations as we know it today.

In March, 1945, 50 participating countries gathered in San Francisco for the "United Nations Conference on International Organization." There, they were presented with a *fait accompli* by the now "Big Five"[3] who had, in advance of the conference, thrashed out the main features and institutional framework of the new international system. The smaller nations, after much chafing and negotiation, grudgingly accepted the inevitable: a "United

---

2. "The Declaration by United Nations" (1942).
3. The United States, the United Kingdom, China, Russia, and France.

Nations dominated by five nations with a veto."[4] All the member states would constitute a General Assembly to debate international issues and approve budgets. There would be a Security Council of five permanent and six non-permanent members, an 18-member Economic and Social Council an International Court of Justice a Trusteeship Council to oversee certain colonial territories, and a Secretariat of international civil servants under a Secretary General. All that remained was to craft the charter containing the preamble, purposes, and principles of the new organization. The charter was approved, signed and came into effect on June 26, 1945, thereby creating the United Nations Organization.

Its role was defined very clearly in the Preamble to the Charter

> We the peoples of the United Nations determined to save succeeding generations from the scourge of war, which twice in our lifetime has brought untold sorrow to mankind, to reaffirm faith in fundamental human rights, in the dignity and worth of the human person, in the equal rights of men and women and of nations large and small, and to establish conditions under which justice and respect for the obligations arising from treaties and other sources of international law can be maintained, and to promote social progress and better standards of life in larger freedom.[5]

It is interesting to note that from the beginning, the violation of human rights was considered a threat to international peace. In this cosmovision, security was seen as a comprehensive global arrangement linked to the promotion and fostering of the social and economic conditions necessary for peace to prevail.[6]

Some seventy years later, the world has changed drastically and the UN is, today, a much bigger and more complex organization, numbering 193 member states and several nonmember states.[7] The Security Council has expanded from 11 to 15 members,

4. Meisler, *United Nations*, 23.
5. UN Charter, Preamble.
6. Weiss, *United Nations in Changing World Politics*, 2.
7. Non-member states include Vatican City, Taiwan, Kosovo, and the

with the addition of four elected, rotating seats. There are dozens of specialized UN agencies and programs and an ever-expanding agenda. So much so that, according to Weiss and his co-authors, there are basically "three United Nations," interacting together in a changing world system. The first is the UN as an organization of sovereign states, meeting together to make international agreements and decisions in the General Assembly, the Security Council, and the Economic and Social Council. The second UN is made up of international civil servants and secretariat staff, headed by the Secretary General, an office that has been held by such outstanding figures as Dag Hammarskjold, Boutros Boutros-Ghali, and Kofi Anan. The third is the UN as the convening center of the world's many nongovernmental organizations and global civil society.[8]

In a recent visit to the United Nations, I heard an alternative, but less scholarly, definition of the "three UNs" provided by members of the NGO community in New York, who refer to them as: "Geneva," "Boots on the Ground," and "The Talk Shop." For the NGOs, the UN offices in Geneva "make things happen," facilitating the organization's work in the promotion of peace, development, and, in particular, human rights; the "Boots on the Ground" are the NGOs themselves, often referred to as the "conscience of the UN," together with their members who are active, at grassroots level, all over the world; while the "Talk Shop" is at the UN in New York, as well as the General Assembly, also described as "the world's noisy but largely toothless town hall"[9] and the Security Council.

Much has changed in the last 70 years, but the politics at the UN, by and large, have not. According to Weiss and his co-authors,[10] knowing the history of the UN is essential for understanding the UN in the present. Its wartime parentage and origins, its legacy of mistrust, interstate diplomatic wrangling, and compromise, together with its delicate balance of power between

---

Palestinian State.

8. Weiss, *United Nations in Changing World Politics*, 3.
9. Patrick, "World Weary, Evaluating the United Nations at 70," 2.
10. Weiss, *United Nations in Changing World Politics*, 4.

the American-led NATO and Warsaw Pact countries, are echoed in the ups and downs of the UN today, where state sovereignty and nation interests do not always yield to the demands for international cooperation to deal with humanitarian disasters. The "Big Five" veto-wielding members of the Security Council have remained unchanged from 1945 and are still resented, while their veto continues to be a highly controversial issue.

Excluded from the Security Council are the losers of World War II, Japan and Germany, which today are the world's third and fourth largest global economies, together with Brazil and India, both emerging economic giants.

Indeed, much of the debate at the UN is permeated by managing these contradictions. But despite its diplomatic crises and machinations, the UN's priorities, even as it faces threats both old and new, are still essentially the three critical themes in international relations: global peace and security, human rights and humanitarian protection, and sustainable development. Here, I intend to limit myself to two of those priorities: the UN's commitment to human rights and humanitarian protection and to the promotion of sustainable development, because these are the issues that engage the passion and the energy of the majority of the NGOs who work with and at the UN, and, in particular, UN-ANIMA International, of which my order is a member.

HUMAN RIGHTS AND HUMAN PROTECTIONS

The basic aim of the founders of the United Nations, as allies in World War II, was the protection of the four essential freedoms proclaimed by President Roosevelt in 1941: "Freedom of speech and of religion, and freedom from want and from fear." After the war, these were determined to include the principles of freedom and human rights in the UN Charter which, accordingly, "reaffirmed faith in fundamental human rights, and dignity and worth of the human person" and committed all member states to promote "universal respect for, and observance of, human rights and fundamental freedoms for all without distinction as to race, sex, language, or religion."[11] The Charter specifically linked human rights to international peace and security, imposing on states the legal obligation to "create conditions of stability and well-being which are necessary for peaceful and friendly relations among nations based on the principle of equal rights and self-determination of peoples."[12]

But when the extent of the Shoah and other atrocities committed by the Nazi regime and imperial Japan during World War II came to light, the language of the Charter was seen as far too vague. Human rights that had, hitherto, been considered a "domestic matter" had become an "urgent international concern."[13] The inalienable rights belonging to every single human being now needed to be defined and promoted in a substantial and sustainable way, which included the responsibility of members of the international community for breaches of internal human rights by other members.

This task fell to the United Nations Economic and Social Council, ECOSOC, set up by the UN Charter to "discharge the functions of the Organization." Among its responsibilities was that of making "recommendations for the purpose of promoting respect for, and observance of, human rights and fundamental freedoms for all."[14] To do so, it was charged with setting up commissions in economic and social fields for the promotion of human rights, and any other commissions it deemed necessary for its work. Accordingly, in 1946 ECOSOC created the UN Commission on Human Rights, chaired by Eleanor Roosevelt. The Commission was entrusted with giving a clearer definition to the abstract ideas expressed in the Charter and drafting an international bill of human rights. By December 1948, the Commission had crafted the Universal Declaration of Human Rights, the first global expression of the rights to which all human beings are inherently entitled. The

11. UN Charter, Preamble and Article 55.
12. UN Charter, Article 55.
13. Volger, Helmut, ed. *A Concise Encyclopedia of the United Nations*. Leiden, Netherlands: Brill, 2012, 257.
14. UN Charter, Article 61 and 62.

Universal Declaration of Human Rights was passed by 48 votes with 8 notable abstentions[15] and was adopted by the United Nations on December 10, 1948.

The Declaration consists of a Preamble and thirty articles. The language of the Preamble is largely a repetition of that of the UN Charter, echoing the same relationship between human rights and world peace:

> Whereas recognition of the inherent dignity and of the equal and inalienable rights of all members of the human family is the foundation of freedom, justice and peace in the world, Whereas disregard and contempt for human rights have resulted in barbarous acts which have outraged the conscience of mankind ... Now, Therefore THE GENERAL ASSEMBLY proclaims THIS UNIVERSAL DECLARATION OF HUMAN RIGHTS as a common standard of achievement for all peoples and all nations.[16]

The Declaration then lists thirty human rights' principles, that cover some sixty basic rights in three main categories: civil and political rights, socio-economic rights, and collective rights, which refer to groups of people rather than to individuals. The Declaration thus established the shape of the contemporary consensus on internationally recognized human rights. The majority of the rights defined are essentially individual rights, each one introduced by the same concept: "All human beings are ...", "Everyone has the right ...", "No one shall be ...", "Everyone is entitled to ..." Eleanor Roosevelt captured the importance and scope of these basic human rights very graphically:

> Where, after all, do universal human rights begin? In small places, close to home—so close and so small that they cannot be seen on any maps of the world. Yet they are the world of the individual person; the neighborhood he lives in; the school or college he attends; the factory,

---

15. The six Soviet bloc states, Saudi Arabia, and South Africa. However, all but Saudi Arabia had renounced their abstention by 1993.

16. Declaration of Human Rights, Preamble.

farm or office where he works. Such are the places where every man, woman, and child seeks equal justice, equal opportunity, equal dignity without discrimination. Unless these rights have meaning there, they have little meaning anywhere. Without concerted citizen action to uphold them close to home, we shall look in vain for progress in the larger world.[17]

The Declaration also offers a holistic approach to human rights; rights that are "universal, indivisible, interdependent and interrelated" as opposed to a list from which "to pick or choose."[18] This approach gives equal status to all rights, while affirming that they interact with one another as a whole to fully respect the dignity of each person. Having adopted the Declaration of Human Rights, the UN member states, despite, or perhaps due to, their ideological and theoretical divergence concerning human rights, decided to work on a more detailed elaboration of two core human rights treaties, one on civil and political rights and the other on social, economic, and cultural rights: the International Covenant on Economic, Social and Cultural Rights, and the International Covenant on Civil and Political Rights, together with their two Optional Protocols. These were completed by 1956, and, together with the Declaration of Human Rights, they constituted the International Bill of Human Rights.

Since then, the Declaration has served as the foundation for other international treaties and conventions in support of human rights: such as the United Nations Convention on the Rights of the Child (1959), the International Convention on the Elimination of All Forms of Racial Discrimination (1965), the International Convention on the Elimination of Discrimination Against Women (1979), the United Nations Convention Against Torture (1984), the United Nations Declaration on the Rights of Indigenous Peoples (2007), and many more. But while all member states endorse "human rights" in theory, approval and ratification

---

17. Eleanor Roosevelt's speech given at the Tenth Anniversary of the Universal Declaration of Human Rights, March 27, 1958.

18. Donnelly, *Universal Human Rights. Theory and Practice*, 28.

of the UN Human Rights' specific agenda has been, and continues to be, a long and difficult process. It was not until 1966 that the states voting in the General Assembly formally approved the two detailed Covenants. Due to member states' jealous protection of their sovereignty and legal independence, it took a further 10 years until, in 1976, after the Covenants had been ratified by a sufficient number of individual nations, they took on the force of international law. But not all member states have signed and ratified all of the human rights' treaties.

One case in point is the US, which is still not yet fully committed to the international human rights system. It has yet to ratify important human rights-related treaties and continues to oppose some forms of international cooperation on human rights such as the International Criminal Court, ICC. However, in 2009, it did sign the Convention on the Rights of Persons with Disabilities, which it has yet to ratify. The other human rights' treaties that the US has not yet signed or ratified are: the International Convention on Economic, Social and Cultural Rights, the Convention of all Forms of Discrimination Against Women, the Convention of the Rights of the Child, and the International Convention on the Protection of the Rights of All Migrant Workers and Members of their Families.

Promoting respect, then, for human rights is a core purpose of the United Nations and has defined its identity as an organization for people around the world, from the very beginning of its existence. Member states, however, continue to bear the primary responsibility for protecting human rights within the domestic jurisdiction of their own countries. Nevertheless, with the acceptance of the International Bill of Human Rights, those rights were "internationalized." But the reality is extremely complex. In today's globalized world with its changing international relations, the distinction between what is domestic and what is international is often blurred. At the same time, compliance with international law and the political will to make a serious and consistent commitment to protect human rights is sometimes lacking in the governmental policies and practice of some member states. Examples abound.

I attended the UN Indigenous Peoples' Forum, celebrated in June 2016, where countless examples were cited of member states either ignoring or actively violating the rights of indigenous peoples. I witnessed so many testimonies of assassinations, displacement of people, sacred lands destroyed, and villages razed to make way for mining companies. Many indigenous groups denounced failures to include them in the political process of the countries where they live. The most moving testimony was the peasant father of one of the Mexican students who had disappeared nearly two years before. Sobbing, he begged the Mexican government to find his son, a request that was ignored. At the closure of the UN Indigenous Peoples' Forum, Ban Ki-moon told the assembled delegates that the UN had heard their cries for help. The UN had done much, he observed, but there was still so much more to do.

A more recent example was reported by the BBC on August 21, 2016:

> An Olympic marathon runner from Ethiopia staged a daring protest against his home government when he crossed the line in Rio on Sunday. Feyisa is from Oromia, home to most of Ethiopia's 35 million Oromo people. Human rights groups say that Ethiopian security forces have killed hundreds of Oromo people in recent weeks as they crack down on anti-government protests.[19]

In order to ensure that states apply the norms set out in the Universal Declaration of Human Rights the United Nations has put in place a monitoring process, using all the resources at its disposal, including its moral authority, diplomatic creativity, and operational reach. It is a broad and complex system that consists of a variety of UN organs and agencies. Their role is usually indirect.

---

19. Oromos are an ethnic majority in Ethiopia that have been historically marginalized and persecuted by the federal government. In 2016, the group was holding protests over the government's plan to reallocate its land, and hundreds—some even say thousands—of those protesters have been killed by government-run security forces.

They "encourage, prod, push, and sometimes embarrass states to take active steps to promote and protect human rights."[20]

The Security Council plays an important part in the protection of rights. It has the authority, by virtue of chapter 7 of the UN Charter, to link the violation of human rights to international peace and security and to order direct intervention in those situations or to declare that economic, judicial, or military steps are needed to correct human rights problems. Such action was taken in Yugoslavia in 1993, and in Rwanda in 1994, to seek legal justice against those responsible for crimes against humanity by creating two *ad hoc* criminal courts to try persons charged with genocide and crimes against humanity. This led to the setting up of a permanent International Criminal Court (ICC) in 2000. However, the ever-present individual states' national interests have resulted in a failure of the Security Council to achieve a balanced and systematic approach to the protection of human rights. One example, among many, is the January 2007 council resolution sponsored by the United States and the United Kingdom, condemning human rights violations by Myanmar, a military dictatorship, as a threat to international security. The resolution was blocked by Russia and China, on the grounds that they posed no threat to international peace, even though both countries did recognize that violations existed. Later, after Myanmar brutally repressed demonstrations, China blocked a resolution calling for sanctions to be imposed.

The UN General Assembly also protects human rights either by passing resolutions, which are unfortunately non-binding, that condemn violations of human rights or by directing negative publicity towards recalcitrant governments. In 2012, when Russia and China vetoed a Security Council resolution on human rights violations by the Syrian government, the General Assembly passed its own strongly-worded resolution of condemnation and rebuke. Only 12 out of 193 countries voted against the resolution. But consensus is an extremely rare event in the General Assembly. State sovereignty and power politics, an option among many developing countries for compromise rather than confrontation, and an

20. Weiss, *United Nations in Changing World Politics*, 360.

intensified North-South divide, together with a recent new chapter in the Cold War, all hamper decisive action to promote and defend human rights.

The Secretary General of the United Nations can also publicly "name and shame" governments responsible for the violation of human rights. But until 1997, the Secretary General "did not publicly display a major commitment to human rights."[21] In that year Kofi Annan, the seventh Secretary General, and a diplomat committed to the values enshrined in the UN Charter, took office. Among his priority concerns were the encouragement of and advocacy for human rights. In 1998, at a ceremony to mark the fiftieth anniversary of the Declaration of Human Rights, he shared his concerns:

> Our belief in the centrality of human rights to the work and life of the United Nations stems from a simple proposition: that States that respect human rights respect the rules of international society. States which respect human rights are more likely to seek cooperation and not confrontation, tolerance and not violence, moderation and not might, peace and not war. States which treat their own people with fundamental respect are more likely to treat their neighbors with the same respect. From this proposition, it is clear that human rights—in practice as in principle—can have no walls and no boundaries.[22]

Practice has proven Kofi Annan's words true, time and time again. His successor, Ban Ki-moon, the eighth General Secretary, a cautious man with a less confrontational approach, also publicly denounced human rights violations.

On June 2, 2016, Reuters Press reported that the UN Secretary-General, Ban Ki-moon, had "slammed the Saudi Arabia-led coalition fighting in Yemen for killing and maiming children, by adding it to an annual blacklist of states and armed groups that violate children's rights during conflict." Saudi Arabia's response

---

21. Weiss, *United Nations in Changing World Politics*, 196.

22. Address to the United Nations Educational, Scientific and Cultural Organization (UNESCO), December 8, 1998.

was the threat to cut Palestinian aid and other UN funding. Its name was, predictably, withdrawn from the blacklist.

But the principal organ that the UN set up in 1946 to fulfill its Charter mandate of respect for human rights and its primary forum for "naming and shaming" states who abused their own citizens was the Commission on Human Rights (CHR). Initially, the Commission was made up of 18 members, elected by ECOSOC, and its first chairperson was Eleanor Roosevelt. With a very broad mandate, the Commission was primarily occupied with standard setting, preparing the Declaration of Human Rights and drafting other human rights declarations. The Commission also set up an extensive network of monitoring mechanisms,[23] to ensure the implementation of those standards. The Commission was effective at this time and emerged as the "United Nations' most important general political and policy body and forum for discussion in the field of Human Rights."[24]

The growing international interest in and concern for human rights led to a steady growth in numbers until the Commission eventually comprised 53 members, some of whom "sought membership of the Commission not to strengthen human rights but to protect themselves from criticism or to criticize others."[25] At the same time, the Commission began to fall from grace as it was perceived to be increasingly involved in double standards, engaging in what James H. Leobvic called "politics of shame"[26] and characterized by non-action.

So much so that "when private complaints about rights violations came to the UN, the CHR buried them in an elaborate process leading nowhere, one of the most complicated trash baskets ever devised. The early Commission, in the words of one careful

23. These mechanisms included reporting procedures, working groups, special rapporteurs, independent experts, field operations, and complaints procedures.

24. Schrijver, "UN Human Rights Council," 812.

25. "Report of the High-Level Panel on Threats, Challenges and Change," UN Doc A/59/565 92204, 283. https://www.un.org/ruleoflaw/files/gaA.59.565_En.pdf.

26. See Leobvic and Voeten, "Politics of Shame."

observer, displayed a "fierce commitment to inoffensiveness."[27] James Lebovic confirms this observation: "The UNCHR selectively enforced rules to support friends and punished adversaries."[28] For a brief period, between 1967 until 1970, the Commission began to examine complaints more seriously and later, during the Cold War, it continued to struggle to find ways of working more effectively, even while its politics became more contentious, often pitting East against West and North against South. Membership of the Commission became highly politicized. In 2002, the United States lost its seat, being in effect voted off of the CHR by the other member states. In 2003, the chairmanship of the Commission was assumed by Libya, while in 2004, Sudan was elected to the Commission, prompting heavy criticism for having countries with poor human rights records, not only as members but as officers. Repeated calls for reform followed.

In April 2005, Kofi Annan, in a speech to the Commission, delivered a breathtaking indictment: "We have reached a point at which the Commission's declining credibility has cast a shadow on the reputation of the United Nations system as a whole, and where piecemeal reforms will not be enough."[29] The Secretary General proposed that the Commission be abolished and replaced by a smaller Human Rights Council (UNHCR) which would be a subsidiary body of the General Assembly, and would work closely with the Office of the High Commissioner for Human Rights. The Human Rights Council (UNHRC) was voted, overwhelmingly, into existence on March 15, 2006, as a key component of the reform process, giving the United Nations, in the words of the Secretary General, "a much-needed chance to make a new beginning in its work for human rights around the world."[30]

27. Weiss, *United Nations in Changing World Politics*, 192.

28. Leobvic and Voeten, "Politics of Shame," 162.

29. Address to UNCHR Geneva (April 2005): https://www.un.org/press/en/2005/sgsm9808.doc.htm

30. UN News. "Palestine refugee crisis 'expanding'; leaving highest number at risk this century across Gaza." un.org/apps/news/story.asp?NEWSID=17811#.WFXqEbYrLqo.

The new Human Rights Council would be slightly smaller than its predecessor and numbering 47 members elected by the UN General Assembly by secret ballot, taking into account their human rights' records. The term on the council would be for three years, and no member state could occupy a seat for more than two consecutive terms. The seats were to be distributed equitably between the regional groups at the UN as follows: 13 for Africa, 13 for Asia, 6 for Eastern Europe, 8 for Latin America and the Caribbean, and 7 for the Western Europe and other groups. The General Assembly reserved the right, via a two-thirds majority, to suspend any council member that it decided had persistently committed gross and systematic violations of human rights during its term of membership. To this end, universal periodic reviews of members' human rights' records would be made during terms of membership. The duration and frequency of the council meetings would be extended, with the possibility of special meetings in urgent cases. And, notably, the voice of NGOs was included through participation and consultation in particular, with regard to the provision of reliable information for the universal periodic reviews (UPRs).

The creation of the Human Rights Council generated high expectations that it would, with these tighter membership requirements, avoid the selectivity, bias, and partiality of its predecessor. Indeed, paragraph 4 of the General Assembly Resolution 60.251, which brought the Council into existence, directs that it "shall be guided by the principles of universality, impartiality, objectivity and non-selectivity, constructive international dialogue and cooperation." But its appearance also generated not a little skepticism, aptly characterized by the title of Schrijver's article: "The UH Human Rights Council: 'A Society of the Committed' or just Old Wine in New Bottles."[31]

Unfortunately, in practice, controversies, polarization, and politicization undermined the Human Rights Council at the outset and throughout its formative years. So much so that the new body was beginning to resemble the one it had replaced. *The New York Times* reported that one political bloc, namely the Organization

---

31. Schrijver, "UN Human Rights Council."

The History, the Mandate and the Working of the UN

of Islamic Cooperation, "stymied Western efforts to direct serious attention to situations like the killings, rape and pillage in the Darfur region of Sudan" in order to focus on the Palestinian cause and the investigation of Israel. The report continues: "The Council has passed eight resolutions against Israel, and the Islamic group is planning four more for the current session. The Council has cited no other country for human rights violations."[32]

But, gradually, the Human Rights Council did begin to find a balance between competing interests and to evolve into something more equitable. The United States was elected to the council in 2009 and tried rather successfully to reform the council from within, until its UPR happened in 2010, when its domestic international human rights' record was called into question.[33]

A very positive development for the UNHRC is its use of fact-finding commissions and commissions made up of independent experts and the continued use of social rapporteurs. These experts, together with NGOs, serve as the eyes and ears of the UN human rights' system, and can lend unbiased views and intellectual depth that can inform decisions and policy, as the UNHRC continues to face the challenges that often make the protection of human rights elusive.

The work of the UNHRC is supervised in Geneva by the High Commissioner for Human Rights, a post created in 1993 as a result of the UN World Conference on Human Rights in Vienna. This is a post with a vague mandate and no authority. As well as giving an annual report on international human rights at the UN, the Commissioner was required to put in place human rights field missions in different countries as needed. The first High Commissioner, José Ayala-Lasso of Ecuador, practiced quiet diplomacy as did his successor. Not so the passionate Mary Robinson, an experienced diplomat, who became the United Nations High Commissioner for Human Rights on September 12, 1997, bringing to the office a

---

32. Hoge, Warren. "Dismay over New U.N. Human Rights Council." *New York Times* (March 11, 2007). https://www.nytimes.com/2007/03/11/world/11rights.html

33. Weiss, *United Nations in Changing World Politics*, 195.

burning commitment to human rights together with her international experience and the determination to place the human rights agenda at the core of UN activities. Her raising of awareness of human rights' violations and championing of socioeconomic rights soon proved an irritant to many member states, including the US. Under pressure from these countries, Mary Robinson stepped down in 2002. The next High Commissioner, Sergio Vieira de Mello, was tragically killed during a suicide bombing of the UN headquarters in Baghdad in 2003. Subsequent High Commissioners, who have spoken out forcefully for human rights, have continued to generate controversy. The current High Commissioner, Zeid Ra'ad Al-Hussein, appointed in 2014 with a long diplomatic record and a reputation as a human rights' advocate, like the Secretary General, has an all but impossible task: trying to motivate states with very different agendas and priorities to implement human rights without, at the same time, alienating them.

The controversies over human rights policies and the role of the UN still continue unabated. For, unfortunately, despite the acceptance of the International Declaration of Human Rights, the UN's monitoring system and the efforts of the Secretary General and High Commissioner, the violation of human rights by member states and others has continued both consistently and regularly. In the face of what he identified as "systemic failure" to prevent and respond to serious violations of human rights, including the genocide in Rwanda and Srebrenica in 1994 and 1995 and the more recent crisis in CAR and in Syria, the Secretary General, Ban Ki-moon, launched the "Human Rights up Front" initiative in December 2013 to strengthen the UN's work. He addressed the UN General Assembly:

> When we look around us today we see the urgent, even desperate, need to react early and to take effective action before situations get out of control, leading to immense human suffering. If there was ever a time to strengthen United Nations prevention work, it is now. With the Human Rights, up Front initiative and process, we have a tool in our hand, which can make a difference in the lives

of millions of people. It can strengthen a dimension of the UN, which can and should inspire confidence and much-needed hope for the future in today's troubled world.[34]

The "Human Rights up Front" initiative includes training all UN staff on the core purpose of promoting respect for human rights, providing member states with the information needed to respond to human rights violations, and ensuring that UN personnel around the world are more attuned to situations where there is a risk of serious human rights abuses and are equipped for the responsibilities that such potential crises entail.

Above all, citing the frequent lack of broad and timely political support that has, in the past, been a key obstacle to early and effective action to prevent human rights crises, the initiative proposes that member states explore ways of strengthening a collective political will to react and act in the face of serious human rights violations. Will the peoples of the world be holding their breath? Perhaps, and then again, perhaps not!

While the United Nations was shaping the Bill of Human Rights and later wrestling with governments to try to ensure the protection of the human rights and the safety and well-being of their populations, the International Committee of the Red Cross (ICRC) was at work outside of UN structures. Acting on the premise that war was inevitable and, driven by its motto *Inter armas caritas* ("compassion in the midst of battle"), the ICRC was attempting to try to make war less barbaric by drawing up rules for warfare and conducting relief operations. It negotiated a series of treaties for the protection of rights and the relief of human suffering in situations of armed conflict that would form the core of international humanitarian law.

In 1949, in the aftermath of the bitter experiences of World War II, the International Committee of the Red Cross, located in Geneva, in consultation with the international community,

---

34. Secretary General's address to the General Assembly on December 17, 2013: https://www.un.org/sg/en/content/dsg/statement/2013-12-17/deputy-secretary-generals-remarks-briefing-general-assembly-rights.

revised and updated the first three Geneva Conventions of 1864, 1906, 1929, and added a fourth. The Geneva Conventions defined the basic rights of wartime prisoners, both military and civilians; established protections for the wounded and sick; and finally, established protections for the civilians in and around a warzone. "To this end," the Convention stipulated,

> the following acts are and shall remain prohibited at any time and in any place whatsoever with respect to the above-mentioned persons: a) violence to life and person, in particular murder of all kinds, mutilation, cruel treatment and torture; b) taking of hostages; c) outrages upon personal dignity, in particular humiliating and degrading treatment; d) the passing of sentences and the carrying out of executions without previous judgment pronounced by a regularly constituted court, affording all the judicial guarantees which are recognized as indispensable by civilized peoples.[35]

The Geneva Convention was ratified by the governments of the 196 countries who were represented at the conference in Geneva. For the first time in history, civilians in occupied territory were recognized as having a right to humanitarian aid without any adverse distinction founded on race, color, religion or faith, sex, birth or wealth, or any other similar criteria.

However, with the beginning of the Cold War, the nature of armed conflicts changed radically. Most armed conflicts were becoming internal wars or insurgencies perpetrated at times by "freedom fighters" or by terrorists, while hostilities were becoming more and more widespread. Moreover, modern armed conflicts were inflicting an increasingly higher toll on civilians, which brought the need to provide non-combatants with protections in time of strife and, in particular, with humanitarian assistance. In light of these developments, two protocols were added to the Conventions in 1977 that extended the terms of the 1949 Conventions with additional protections. One protocol addressed the rights of the victims of international armed conflict and the second, the

---

35. The Geneva Convention (1949), Article 3.

rights of those in the midst of domestic or internal armed conflict. But in the work of the ICRC, humanitarian law and humanitarian action on behalf of the victims of war are and have always been inextricably linked. In this respect, the UN and the ICRC were, and are, essentially reading from the same human rights' page, if for different reasons.

Following the Cold War, the 1990s witnessed a number of major crises and conflicts. The widespread hostilities all over the world and human rights in situations of armed conflict and civil wars that resulted in massive suffering among civilians, became an increasingly disturbing concern for the United Nations. Genocide, ethnic cleansing, and other major crimes against humanity were witnessed in Rwanda and the Balkans in the 1990s, and again in Darfur and Sri Lanka in the 2000s. Faced with a lack of political solutions to situations of extreme violence and restricted access, the UN found it necessary to redesign its international humanitarian architecture on the basis of new mandates in order to attempt to halt or prevent the suffering of civilians caught up in these situations. Subsequent to a review of capacity and coordination arrangements, on December 19, 1991, the General Assembly passed Resolution 46/182 on the "Strengthening of the coordination of humanitarian emergency assistance of the United Nations." The resolution combined the agencies responsible for humanitarian relief into the Office for the Coordination of Humanitarian Affairs (OCHA), headed by an Under-Secretary General. It also made possible greater UN involvement in internal conflicts. At the same time, as the UN was intensifying its investment in humanitarian action, member states were becoming much more willing to become involved in the organization and delivery of humanitarian aid: "a willingness" as Barnett puts it, which was "owed not only to a newfound passion for compassion but, also, to a belief that their political, economic, and strategic interests were at stake."[36]

---

36. M. Barnett quoted by Eleanor Davey in *History of the Humanitarian System: Western Origins and Foundations*. 2013. https://www.odi.org/sites/odi.org.uk/files/odi-assets/publications-opinion-files/8439.pdf.

Steeped in politics at all levels, the attempts of the UN to coordinate humanitarian aid to civilians in conflict situations faces many challenges. The UN intersects in myriad ways with national governments, with armed insurgents, and with local populations. How and to whom to deliver aid can have significant political consequences, particularly in warzones where aid workers have to confront forces that seek to obstruct assistance for political, economic, and military advantage.

The civil war in Syria is a case in point. Against the background of the vivid reporting on social media of the terrible plight of civilians there, I personally witnessed Stephen O'Brien, the Under-Secretary General for Humanitarian Affairs and Emergency Relief Coordinator, present a well-documented report to the Security Council in May, 2016. In it, he detailed the repeated requests to send aid convoys to deliver food and medicines to sick and starving civilians in besieged cities. He reported that due to the obstructionism of the Syrian government, which had regularly denied permission or, on the three occasions when permission was granted, ordered the removal of the aid en route, the UN had been unable to alleviate the plight of the people. The response of the Syrian authorities, supported by the Russian ambassador, was to reject his report as false. The Security Council Meeting was abandoned without further comment or discussion, by an obviously embarrassed Egyptian presiding officer. The Syrian government has continued to block humanitarian aid to its innocent, starving people, particularly in Aleppo. The UN has continued desperately to create a humanitarian space to treat the victims of this conflict and protect the human right to life.

The OCHA often leads the humanitarian charge in what are called "complex emergencies," but it also tries to coordinate international relief and the countless agencies that contribute assistance, including many NGOs, none of which can claim consistent success in delivering humanitarian aid in these situations. Often these "emergencies" become the backdrops to heartbreak and frustration and even lethal attacks on relief workers. But the acute challenges that the humanitarian action of the UN faces needs the political support of the General Assembly and the Security Council. That support is sometimes lacking or fumbled, involving, as it does, member states whose sovereignty or national interest is perceived to be at stake, or who are using starvation as a weapon or who are engaged in intentional ethnic cleansing or deliberate attacks on civilians. Or, as Weiss claims, "unfortunately, all too often, member states vote for or against a particular UN organization or one of its activities as a diplomatic concession to some domestic group or as part of a compromise with other states."[37] This is true of the OCHA and its work of humanitarian relief.

NGOS AND DEVELOPMENT

The second important dimension of the story of the UN and its commitment to human rights is the priority that it has given to the eradication of poverty and issues around development. Many NGOs feature prominently in this chapter of the UN's narrative. From the start in 1945, one of the main priorities of the United Nations was to achieve international cooperation in solving international problems of an economic, social, cultural, or humanitarian character and to encourage respect for human rights. And even though development is central to the eradication of poverty and inextricably linked to peace, security, and human rights, it began life at the UN largely as an implicit or secondary goal.

In the early years of the UN from 1945–1962, development was construed in terms of national economic development, with important roles attributed to the World Bank and the International Monetary Fund (IMF). Then, during the 1960s, 1970s, and 1980s, as the international political context changed, development was interpreted differently by different groups and took on various diverse meanings. For some, it meant economic growth, for others it included human and social elements, such as the inability of some countries to meet the basic needs of their people. Through the General Assembly and ECOSOC—the UN agency that has

---

37. Weiss, *United Nations in Changing World Politics*, 278.

responsibility for promoting and coordinating UN development activities—the UN worked at building consensus around the evolving and, at times, controversial definitions of development.

With the expansion of the UN, due largely to the global decolonization movement of the 1960s and 1970s, new insights were brought into the causes of underdevelopment and poverty. The UN sought to redress global economic imbalances and provide self-reliance to Third World countries. Gradually, the perspectives of economic growth and environmental protection were fused. In 1987, the Bruntland Commission's report, *Our Common Future*, linked the issues of economic development, environmental stability, and sustainability. "Development that meets the needs of the present without compromising the ability of future generations to meet their own needs."[38]

Over time, and through diplomacy and compromise, the international community arrived at the understanding of development as sustainable human development, with its inherent problems of poverty, inequality, resource depletion, pollution and climate change and their causes, together with a shared commitment to take action.

Various summit conferences were part of this journey. Pope Francis makes reference to some of them with his characteristic realism in his encyclical on the "Care of Our Common Home":

> Recent World Summits on the environment have not lived up to expectations because, due to lack of political will, they were unable to reach truly meaningful and effective global agreements on the environment. The 1992 Earth Summit in Rio de Janeiro is worth mentioning. It proclaimed that "human beings are at the center of concerns for sustainable development. Although the summit was a real step forward, and prophetic for its time, its accords have been poorly implemented, due to the lack of suitable mechanisms for oversight, periodic review and penalties in cases of non-compliance. The principles

---

38. Bruntland Commission, *Our Common Future*, 41. Full text at: http://www.un-documents.net/our-common-future.pdf.

which it proclaimed still await an efficient and flexible means of practical implementation.[39]

Francis continues:

> The Conference of the United Nations on Sustainable Development, "Rio+20" (Rio de Janeiro 2012), issued a wide-ranging but ineffectual outcome document. International negotiations cannot make significant progress due to positions taken by countries which place their national interests above the global common good.[40]

But these conferences, each with its faltering steps, one by one, paved the way for the UN's development goals agenda: the UN strategies for eradicating extreme poverty. The presence of NGOs at these conferences and their input to these strategies was notable. The 2000 "Millennium Declaration" identified eight development challenges and translated them into the Millennium Development Goals (MDGs) for ending poverty, eradicating hunger, achieving universal primary education, improving health, and restoring a healthy environment. Gradually, these goals were expanded to become the Sustainable Development Goals (SDGs) officially known as "Transforming our world: the 2030 Agenda for Sustainable Development," adopted in a final document at the UN Sustainable Development Summit in September 25, 2015, in New York.

Pope Francis addressed the United Nations General Assembly on the same day. He remarked that:

> The adoption of the 2030 Agenda for Sustainable Development at the World Summit, which opens today, is an important sign of hope. I am similarly confident that the Paris Conference on Climatic Change will secure fundamental and effective agreements. Solemn commitments, however, are not enough, although they are certainly a necessary step toward solutions . . . Our world demands of all government leaders a will which is effective, practical and constant, concrete steps and immediate measures for preserving and improving the

---

39. Francis, *Laudato Si*, 205, 167.
40. Francis, *Laudato Si*, 169.

natural environment and thus putting an end as quickly as possible to the phenomenon of social and economic exclusion, with its baneful consequences.[41]

Perhaps the member states were moved the Pope's words. At any rate, three months later, a landmark agreement was reached in Paris, December 2015. A global consensus, negotiated by the representatives of 195 countries, to take concrete, verifiable steps to reduce greenhouse gas emissions starting in 2020, was reached. Furthermore, the international community has continued to take practical steps to address climate change. The BBC reported on October 15, 2016 that a "monumental deal" had been reached in Kigali, Rwanda, by 150 nations to phase out gases that are making global warming worse by cutting back their use of hydrofluorocarbons (HFCs) widely used in fridges, air conditioning, and aerosol sprays, from 2019.[42]

The United Nations has achieved much. In the words of Francis:

> The history of this organized community of states is one of important common achievements over a period of unusually fast-paced changes. Without claiming to be exhaustive, we can mention the codification and development of international law, the establishment of international norms regarding human rights, advances in humanitarian law, the resolution of numerous conflicts, operations of peace-keeping and reconciliation, and any number of other accomplishments in every area of international activity and endeavor. All these achievements are lights which help to dispel the darkness of the disorder caused by unrestrained ambitions and collective forms of selfishness.[43]

---

41. Pope Francis's address to the United Nations General Assembly, September 25, 2015: http://w2.vatican.va/content/francesco/en/speeches/2015/september/documents/papa-francesco_20150925_onu-visita.html.

42. McGrath, Matt. "Climate change: 'Monumental' deal to cut HFCs, fastest growing greenhouse gases." *BBC News* (October 15, 2016): https://www.bbc.com/news/science-environment-37665529.

43. Pope Francis's address to the United Nations General Assembly,

The United Nations is built around three critical themes in international relations:

1. international peace and security,
2. human rights and humanitarian relief and protection, and
3. sustainable human development.

Its work over the years has improved the lives and dignity of millions of people. Indeed, without the United Nations the world would undoubtedly be a much worse place. But the organization does have its deficiencies. It is only as strong or as weak as "We, the People of the United Nations," or the first UN entity, choose to make it. With major powers and government groupings constantly disagreeing and fighting each other, and in an international context where, unfortunately, sovereignty and national interest often trump the common good, the UN is only as good as its 193 parts.

So this is the United Nations, with its live theater where the drama of human rights and sustainable development is played out. This is the space where the Handmaids of the Sacred Heart of Jesus have chosen to do public theology. Their choice is to do so as a member of an NGO. The story of how the relationship between the UN and the NGOs has developed over the years places the work of the Handmaids of the Sacred Heart in a larger context. And that is what the next chapter in our narrative is about.

September 25, 2015: http://w2.vatican.va/content/francesco/en/speeches/2015/september/documents/papa-francesco_20150925_onu-visita.html.

Chapter 4

Non-Governmental Organizations (NGOs) and the United Nations

AS WE HAVE SEEN, the United Nations, is really three different yet interactive entities that are meant to cooperate but can also work at cross purposes. The "third UN", now increasing called "civil society," is the network of certain NGOs, external experts, academics, and consultants, who regularly engage and work closely with the first and second UN. They have two roles within UN politics: they are advocates and they are "boots on the ground." Weiss describes their contribution thus: "They represent an important lobbying force for policies or changes in existing policy developed by the first and second UN. They do this by providing collecting, and disseminating data and through advocacy."[1] Members of the third UN are particularly well-placed to present cutting-edge ideas, shifts in priorities, and unbiased policies, because they are not working for governments nor are they international civil servants. Weiss continues: "Secondly, NGOs play a subcontracting role in delivering humanitarian and development aid . . . The NGOs also perform a crucial monitoring role and assess the status of human rights

---

1. Weiss, *United Nations in Changing World Politics*, 5.

and humanitarian principles as well as progress on development indicators or environmental conditions."[2]

The important ongoing relationship between the UN and NGOs has been part of the history of the UN from the very beginning. "In addition to the 5,000 government delegates, members of the media, and other officials and staff at the founding conference of the United Nations in San Francisco in 1945, some 1,500 participants came from nongovernmental organizations (NGOs)."[3] Those NGOs successfully advocated for the inclusion of human rights in the UN Charter and for the adoption of the International Declaration of Human Rights three years later.

Article 71 of the UN Charter explicitly made room for NGOs in the corridors of the UN, providing a legal basis for their participation in UN debates:

> The Economic and Social Council may make suitable arrangements for consultation with non-governmental organizations which are concerned with matters within its competence. Such arrangements may be made with international organizations and, where appropriate, with national organizations after consultation with the Member of the United Nations concerned.

This groundbreaking provision allowed the Economic and Social Council (ECOSOC) to engage in consultative relationships with NGOs. Effectively, it authorized ECOSOC to grant "consultative status" to NGOs. Consultative status is requested by each NGO and, if granted, enables the accredited organizations, within certain parameters, to attend meetings of ECOSOC and the Human Rights Council alongside governmental delegations, and to present oral and written interventions on agenda items. It even allows NGOs to propose items for the agendas, but without giving them

2. Weiss, *United Nations in Changing World Politics*, 6. As I write, UNANIMA International has been asked to provide data on several countries whose human rights record is being assessed for their Universal Periodic Review (UPR).

3. UN Intellectual History Project, "What is the Third United Nations?" Briefing Note 3 (May 2009). http://www.unhistory.org/briefing/3ThirdUN.pdf.

a right to vote. In 1946, NGOs took part in formal UN deliberations through ECOSOC for the first time. By 1948, there were already 45 NGOs with consultative status at the UN. The criteria for NGO accreditation for consultative status have been revised several times, most recently in 1996. The 1996 ECOSOC resolution agreed on more flexible NGO accreditation standards, envisaging a "broad-based participation" by NGOs within ECOSOC and its functional commissions, such as the Human Rights Commission and the Commission on Sustainable Development (CSD). The resolution also detailed the participation of NGOs at international UN-sponsored conferences that had become routine since the Stockholm Conference in 1972. Since then, the presence of NGOs at conferences has mushroomed, as evidenced by the 17,000 NGO participants at the 1992 Earth Summit in Rio and the 32,000 at the 1995 women's conference in Beijing. They were present in droves at the Millennium Summit, the 2005 World Summit, Rio+20 in 2012, and the Paris Climate Change Conference in 2015.

There has been a substantial increase in the number of organizations with consultative status at the UN from 41 in 1946 to 4,665 in 2016. Indeed, "the proliferation of NGOs," according to Claude Welch, Jr., "has been one of the most striking features of contemporary international politics."[4] This increase has been attributed partly to the accelerating pace of globalization, along with the revolution in information and communication technology. At the same time, in a world where economic crises, armed conflict, public health emergencies, food insecurity, and climate change are all threatening the realization of human rights, together with the alarming intensification of inequality, human rights are continually forgotten, neglected, and violated. In this context, concludes Welch, "while states remain the major protectors—and abusers—of human rights, NGOs have emerged as central players in the promotion of human rights around the world."[5]

NGOs work in partnership with the UN at consultative, deliberative, and implementation levels for its policies, priorities, and

4. Welch, *NGOs and Human Rights Promise and Performance*, 1.
5. Welch, *NGOs and Human Rights Promise and Performance*, 1.

actions, often contributing valuable information and ideas. Much of their engagement with the UN takes place at its headquarters in both New York and Geneva, where they serve on multiple UN commissions, attending sessions of UN committees and submitting written and oral statements or interventions. Often those sessions are interminable, lasting all day and into the early hours of the morning. Occasionally it is only then, at first light, that NGOs manage to make their interventions!

They also participate in debates, interactive dialogues, panel discussions, and informal meetings within the UN. They regularly attend UN briefings and convene side events on current issues that provide an opportunity for education and discussion. In addition, NGOs are involved at the UN through networking and advocacy. This type of interaction includes activities and initiatives that come from NGOs and are directed either towards the public, other NGOs, or UN players: public lectures, movie screenings, exhibitions, media statements, and interviews. NGOS frequently build networks, coalitions, and working groups around important or urgent issues in order to lobby more effectively and to combine forces to "push for new policies, and mobilize public opinion around UN deliberations and operations."[6] An important strategy for NGOs is visiting, interacting with, and lobbying member states' missions in formal or informal settings.

In particular, specialized NGOs make significant contributions to promoting and protecting human rights and humanitarian principles, above all through advocacy. In the field, they provide essential operational capacity in emergencies and development efforts. They complement and, at times, challenge existing human rights policy and humanitarian diplomacy by putting pressure on member states and the second UN and by "naming and shaming" those states who violate rights and impede NGOs in their humanitarian relief work. Two of the most well-known NGOs who work with the UN are Amnesty International and Franciscans International. Amnesty International (AI) with its motto: "It is better to light a candle than to curse the darkness," has been an accredited

6. Weiss et al., "Third United Nations," 123.

NGO at the UN since 1964. AI claims: "Through our detailed research and determined campaigning we help fight abuses of human rights worldwide. We bring torturers to justice, change oppressive laws, and free people jailed just for voicing their opinion."[7] Since 1989, Franciscans International has been a "Franciscan voice at the United Nations, protecting the vulnerable, the forgotten and our wounded earth through advocacy."[8]

The value of cooperation with NGOs and their input has been widely recognized particularly by the "second UN." Viru Dayal, former assistant to two Secretaries General, commented: "I think life would be duller without the NGOs, and there would probably be much less point to it also. Besides, civil society knows where the shoe pinches. They know when to laugh and they know when to cry."[9] In 1995, the UN Under-Secretary-General Desai, described the interaction of NGOs with the UN in these terms: "NGOs . . . have increasingly assumed the role of promoters of new ideas, they have alerted the world community to emerging issues, and they have developed expertise and talent which . . . have become vital for the work of the United Nations, both at the policy and operational levels."[10]

Boutros Boutros Ghali himself hailed NGOs as "an essential part of the legitimacy without which no international activity can be meaningful."[11] Addressing the NGO representatives at the UN directly, in September 1994, he said:

> I want you to consider this your home. Until recently, these words might have caused astonishment. The United Nations was considered to be a forum for sovereign

7. Amnesty International, "What We Do." https://www.amnesty.org/en/what-we-do/.
8. Franciscans International. https://franciscansinternational.org/home/.
9. Weiss et al., "Third United Nations," 123.
10. Weiss et al., "Third United Nations," 123.
11. Boutros-Ghali, Boutros. "Democracy, A Newly-Recognized Imperative." *Global Governance* 1.1. (1995), 3–11. Cited by Cyril Ritchie, "Changing Relations Between International Non-Governmental Organizations and the United Nations, Union of International Associations." http://www.uia.org/archive/ingos-un.

states alone. Within the space of a few short years, this attitude has changed. Non-governmental organizations are now considered full participants in international life. . . . Thank you very much for all you have been doing for humanity. Thank you for everything you do to support the United Nations.[12]

Secretary General, Ban Ki Moon also valued the voices and views of NGOs: he remarked in October 2011:

> We simply could not do without your passion, your ideas, and your criticism, too. . . . And I am committed to doing what I can to nurture and deepen this UN-NGO relationship. In our modern world, so complex and fast-changing, no nation or institution can prosper alone. Only by working in concert, in strong partnership, can we advance our common goals.[13]

But inevitably, as with everything at the UN, conflict, controversy, and politicization were never far away. As early as 2006, the Global Policy Forum (GPF) opined:

> Given the diverse nature and large number of NGOs, relations between NGOs and the UN have, at times, been stormy. NGOs face a constant battle to be heard at the UN, and often must compete with businesses and other private sector organizations toward which the UN is increasingly friendly.
>
> While some NGOs enjoy excellent access to meetings and good relations with UN officials and delegations, governments sometimes react negatively to NGO advocacy and seek to restrict NGO opportunities.[14]

---

12. Boutros Boutras-Ghali's address to NGO representatives at UN, September 1994.

13. Ban Ki-moon, "Remarks to Non-Governmental Organizations," October 26, 2011: https://www.un.org/sg/en/content/sg/speeches/2011-10-26/remarks-non-governmental-organizations.

14. Global Policy Forum. "Relations between NGOs and the UN." 2006. https://www.globalpolicy.org/ngos/ngos-and-the-un/31838.html.

The GPF, accordingly, presented an official submission to the President of the UN General Assembly, requesting that the UN should not reduce existing rights and responsibilities and forms of NGO access and participation but, rather, should honor NGO rights stipulated in the ECOSOC resolution of 1996/31 and in recognition of the value of cooperation with NGOs at all levels in UN policies and actions.

In a paper written during an internship program at the ECOSOC office in 2011, Lisa Bostrom identified the NGOs that were experiencing difficulties at the UN as organizations who represented issues that were sensitive to some member states, in particular human rights issues. After stating that in her opinion, "the work of the Committee on NGOs is much politicized," she goes on to say that "independent Human Rights organizations that criticize member states, for human rights violations, have difficulty getting status, or, if they already have status, member states try to silence them by intimidation or by having their status withdrawn."[15] Bostrom is not alone in the realistic conclusions she draws: "One cannot overlook the fact that the intergovernmental body will inevitably reflect the dynamics and international relations between different member states. It would be naïve to expect states to overlook their national interests in the NGO Committee as much as in any other part of the United Nations system."[16]

I personally heard similar stories, murmurs, and fears while participating at the UN Indigenous Forum in May 2016. I attended meetings of the NGO Committee and witnessed several NGOs denied status. Ban Ki-moon added his own concerns to the growing chorus at the Non-Governmental Organizations Conference in Seoul in 2016. He indicated that he was deeply disappointed that the member states on the ECOSOC NGO Committee had recently denied the Committee to Protect Journalists consultative status. He added that he was also opposed to the exclusion of LGBT organizations from the upcoming High-Level Meeting on Ending AIDS. "These NGOs are close to communities affected by

---

15. Bostrom, *Controversial Issues in the NGO Committee*, 7.
16. Bostrom, *Controversial Issues in the NGO Committee*, 7.

the epidemic and they must be part of the response," he stated.[17] Denouncing the shrinking of "democratic space" at the UN, he urged freedom for civil society organizations, NGOs, and human rights defenders, noting that unfortunately, such freedom is under threat, "including at the last place this should happen: at the United Nations."

The UN has always been a blend of ideals and reality: striving for a better world, a world of peace, justice, equality, and sustainable prosperity for all, where human rights are universally recognized and protected; and, at the same time, the UN is haunted by the failure to make that dream come true. In a world where too many people are suffering too much, the majority of the NGOs who work in partnership with the UN share the same dream to eradicate global poverty and inequality that threaten world peace, and they are committed to doing all they can to make that dream come true.

Strolling along the corridors of the United Nations headquarters in New York, especially when the General Assembly is in session or a UN event is happening, it is not unusual to see a few saffron-robed monks or a woman in a hijab, a turbaned Sikh or a Jew wearing a kippah, an occasional habited nun, or men and women sporting clerical collars, crosses of all sizes, congregational pins, and various other religious insignia. All of them are evidence of the ubiquitous presence of "faith-based" or religious NGOs (RNGOs) that attend, work, and pray at the UN. Research[18] estimates that of the 4,665 NGOs with consultative status with ECOSOC, approximately 320 are RNGOs. While they represent many faith traditions, just under half of them (151) are Christian and of those over 50 percent are Catholic, 40 percent are Protestant, and 8 percent are called by the designation "other Christians." Other religious affiliations represented are: Muslims (13 percent with

17. Ban Ki-moon, "SG's remarks at opening of the 66th UN DPI/NGO Conference," May 30, 2016: https://www.un.org/sg/en/content/sg/statement/2016-05-30/secretary-generals-remarks-opening-66th-un-dpingo-conference.

18. See the University of Kent Project, 2009–2012. http://erb.unaoc.org/wp-content/uploads/2014/01/UN-NGO-Report-4.pdf.

32 RNGOs), Jewish (9 percent with 29 RNGOs), self-identified as "spiritual" (11 percent with 24 RNGOs), multi-religious (5 percent with 13 RNGOs), Buddhist (4 percent with 10 RNGOs), Bahai (2 percent with 2 RNGOs), and Hindu and Jain, (both 1 percent with 1 RNGO).

Although the United Nations is essentially a secular organization, historically it was inspired by the religious heritage of the West. Indeed, religious groups have been actively collaborating with the UN since the beginning and have seriously influenced the language of its foundational documents. For example, Frederick Nolde, dean of the graduate school at the Lutheran Theological Seminary at Philadelphia, together with Judge Joseph Proskauer and Jacob Blaustein, both Jewish, led efforts to lobby for the inclusion of human rights and fundamental freedoms in both the Charter and the International Declaration of Human Rights. "The effect of this intervention" according to Robert Traer,

> was that the rights of individuals, as well as the rights of nations, will be incorporated in the San Francisco Charter it was learned today, largely as the result of the efforts of a Philadelphia clergyman Nolde, who was a professor in the Lutheran Theological Seminary.[19]

Traer also attributes an important part in the formulation of the draft International Declaration of Human Rights to Monsignor Roncalli, who was the papal nuncio in Paris at the time and who subsequently became Pope John XXIII.

With the International Declaration of Human Rights as the foundation for a worldwide effort in the promotion and enforcement of human rights, and once Article 71 of the United Nations Charter had created a political space for civil society to be part of those efforts, it was to be assumed that both secular and religious groups would flock to the United Nations to request consultative status in order to inject their voice into public debate and policy discussions on issues of human rights, sustainable development,

---

19. Traer, "Universal Declaration of Human Rights," *The Philadelphia Inquirer* (May 4, 1945). http://religionhumanrights.com/Law/UDHR/cornerstone.fhr.htm.

the environment, peacebuilding, and governance. At the same time, given their international networks of human resources, the NGOs and RNGOs offered extensive relief and social services in many regions of the world. For RNGOs this meant simply continuing the long history of their widespread humanitarian work, caring for the vulnerable and disadvantaged that has characterized faith traditions throughout history: Catholic hospitals, Islamic foundations and Buddhist monasteries, among many others, have consistently provided aid to the poor. Today the majority of RNGOs are involved in activities related to social and economic development, social justice, and humanitarian aid, which include peace building, relief, education, health, environment protection, culture, and human rights.

Successive UN World Conferences and summits have also raised further the awareness of religious NGOs of the importance of the UN as a stage for decision-making and motivated their engagement with the organization as actors on that stage, either positively or, at times, negatively. The Conference on Population and Development in 1994, in particular, proved controversial, drawing in many Catholic and Muslim NGOs that generated a heated debate on reproductive rights. Six years later, the Millennium World Summit represented "a new partnership between religious and political institutions working to renew human compassion, end the desperation of hunger and poverty and secure greater peace."[20]

According to Julia Berger, RNGOs are "a unique hybrid of religious beliefs and socio-political activism at all levels of society."[21] They are driven by an explicitly public mission that is motivated by their faith convictions, often expressed in their mission statements, that outline the overall purpose of the NGOs and their underlying values and principles. They all reflect one basic theme—an unshakable recognition and vigorous defense of the God-given dignity and sacred nature of human life and the rights of the human person.

---

20. Berger, "Religious NGOs at the United Nations," 3.
21. Berger, "Religious NGOs at the United Nations," 1.

Catholics and other Christian traditions obviously follow Jesus Christ in their work for justice with the poor and oppressed. Catholic Relief Services, one of the largest RNGOs at the UN, clearly states the biblical basis of its commitment: "The fundamental motivating force in all activities of CRS is the Gospel of Jesus Christ, as it pertains to the alleviation of human suffering, the development of people and the fostering of charity and justice in the world." Non-Christian RNGOs are similarly motivated by their beliefs. Many Muslim RNGOs refer to the Qu'ran as well as to the sayings of the Prophet Muhammad, expressing a religious duty to help those in need. Jewish organizations often refer to the Jewish principle of *tikkun olam,* as well as the social justice teachings in the Torah. Buddhist and Hindu RNGOs also highlight their particular religious values in their mission statements.

Of particular significance for Catholic organizations was Vatican II which, in its landmark document *Gaudium et Spes,* defined the Catholic Church's relationship with the modern world in terms of solidarity: "The joys and the hopes, the griefs and the anxieties of the people of this age, especially those who are poor or in any way afflicted, these are the joys and hopes, the griefs and anxieties of the followers of Christ."[22] This description of the role of the Church in the world marked a major development in the understanding of the place of the work for justice in the mission of the Church. The ongoing development of Catholic social teaching also profoundly impacted Catholic organizations' understanding of their role in the international arena, as did the birth of both public theology and liberation theology.

RNGOs, whether from liberal or conservative platforms, are engaged with the UN on various levels with a varying degree of visibility. Like secular NGOs, they rely to a large extent on advocacy and lobbying to influence debates and decision-making and to address world problems at the systemic level, and to collaborate on international issues of common concern. Many of the smaller organizations operate jointly through NGO committees and other networks to increase their impact. Founded

---

22. Vatican II, *Gaudium et Spes,* 1.

in 1972, the Committee of RNGOs at the United Nations is one such coalition of representatives of religious, spiritual and ethical non-governmental organizations who meet regularly to exchange varying points of view and promote networking. They also host interreligious prayer services related to UN events and campaigns.

Kofi Annan paid tribute to the work of RNGOs in 2006, when speaking at the Church of the Holy Family:

> Men and women of faith are crucial to the United Nations. As teachers and guides, you can be agents of change and inspire people to new levels of public service. You can help bridge the chasms of ignorance, fear, and misunderstanding that plague our world. You can set an example of inter-faith dialogue, co-operation and respect. My great predecessor, Dag Hammarskjold once said, and I quote: 'The United Nations stands outside—necessarily outside—all confessions. But, it is inspired by what unites and not by what divides the great religions of the world.'[23]

Among the groups of Catholic non-governmental organizations at the United Nations are religious institutes of men and women, who have come to see the United Nations as a key arena of advocacy on behalf of those they serve. Most of them have a very long tradition of commitment to those living in poverty and of direct service to the people living on the margins and the underside of society all over the world. Given the enormity and complexity of the suffering in contemporary society, religious men and women have seen the importance of identifying and addressing the systemic causes of deepening poverty and ever-increasing inequality which are embedded in unjust social structures. Responding to the call of Vatican II to a radical renewal of religious life based on the spirit or charisms of their founders and foundresses, and the call to read the "signs of the times," many religious institutes made a profound paradigm shift in their ministry to focus on the poor and disadvantaged. A new sense of mission and a call to do justice on a completely different level emerged as they began looking for

---

23. Annan, *Universal Religious Values Animate UN,* September, 2006.

new ways to become more effective agents of change by promoting justice on the ground and to bring about structural change.

At the same time, they recognized that the vision of the United Nations Organization as stated in its Charter and, especially, in the Preamble, paralleled the foundational aims of their own religious institutes. As global men and women impelled by the gospel agenda with hearts that embrace the whole world, and committed to social justice issues that do not stop at any borders, Catholic Sisters, Brothers, and priests decided to invest in ministry at the UN; a ministry that would enable them to live a more dynamic renewal of their original charisms and to announce the gospel in a new place in a new way. Their relationship with the UN was characterized by a two-way dialogue. As NGOs associated with the Department of Public Information (DPI), they are able to communicate between the UN offices and the men and women religious in the field. In addition, thanks to their consultative status with ECOSOC, they can communicate from those in the field with the UN, and in this way ground global advocacy in the local activities of the members of their religious institutes.

Religious institutes also recognized that working with other like-minded groups at the United Nations offered an opportunity to be effective advocates for more just global structures and a shared universal solidarity. While they have much in common, and all believe that working for justice is constitutive of the gospel, each religious community brings its own original gift and specific reading of the gospel to its work at the UN. Each one has its own corporate stance and specific experience, strengthened by analysis and prayerful reflection, to bring to the negotiating table. To cite just a few: the Passionists'[24] commitment to justice is based on their worldview of an international society where increasing numbers of poor people are being 'crucified' by unjust and economic structures. "The passion and death of Jesus" they hold "are no mere historical events. They are ever present realties to people in the

---

24. The Passionists are a religious order of priests and Brothers, founded by St. Paul of the Cross.

world of today, 'crucified' as they are by injustice."[25] The Medical Missionary Sisters see their involvement at the UN as an extension of their healing mission in a wounded world. The Religious Sisters of Mercy's (RSM) focus is especially on women and children.

All members of religious communities are present at the UN to knock on diplomats' doors, urging them to listen to the people's voices. Many of them actively voice the concerns of the voiceless that are living in poverty. Some use their financial resources to bring those living in poverty to the offices at the UN to speak for themselves, believing that the ability to make one's voice heard at the UN empowers people. So often the UN debates tend to lean towards political interests, all the while forgetting to place people at the center of the debate.

Members of religious communities are usually highly skilled professionals. They often inhabit multicultural worlds. They know how to dialogue across differences and are used to working in collaboration with others. At the UN they belong to several networks. They attend both the Committee of RNGOs and the International Catholic Organization (ICO), which equally provide support and opportunities for sharing experiences. But RUN, Religious at the UN, is a support group specifically for members of religious congregations, each with their own needs and their different charisms, but all sharing a common mission as NGOs at the UN. RUN provides religious men and women with opportunities for theological discussions and prayer. Religious congregations also form coalitions made up of federations of the same religious family, or sometimes smaller congregations join with others to form a RNGO, as in the case of UNANIMA International.

All RNGOs face many challenges and competing realities at the United Nations. They witness the many controversies, both political and social, that identify the UN like fingerprints. But they are there, while members of religious congregations are tenaciously there. Joseph C. Donnelly, Permanent Delegate to the United Nations of Caritas Internationalis, writes: "The Community of Catholic sisters, brothers, and priests are present at the UN everyday

25. Obiezu, *It is Good for Us to Be Here*, 40.

through its many uncertain seasons in New York and Geneva—as they do in remote places and major cities all around the world."[26] According to Professor Joy U. Ogwu, the Nigerian ambassador to the United Nations, religious institutes are "the most influential faith-based NGOs. They have not only played a range of positive roles but have also affected UN decision making and its approach to global issues by the moral and ethical consciousness they bring to the entire process of peace, security and development."[27] The Handmaids of the Sacred Heart are now part of that process.

---

26. Obiezu, *It is Good for Us to Be Here*, 68.
27. Obiezu, *It is Good for us to Be Here*, 2.

Chapter 5

Handmaids of the Sacred Heart of Jesus

THE CONGREGATION OF THE Handmaids of the Sacred Heart of Jesus was founded in Spain, in 1877, by Rafaela Maria Porras and her sister Dolores. The birth of the institute was situated in Madrid, the heart of Spanish society, in the late nineteenth century, at a time when the previous political and civil unrest and social degeneration had resulted in an urgent need for comprehensive social reform. In this context, the genesis of the new institute's commitment to the poor and disadvantaged is to be found in the life and the dreams of Rafaela Maria Porras, known today as St. Raphaela.

Raphaela was born in 1850 in Pedro Abad, a small Andalusian town; at this time Spain was agitated by new concerns born of an era of liberalism. According to the primitive writings of the institute, they were "calamitous times,"[1] continually alternating between conservative or progressive revolutions. There was a widespread anti-Catholic spirit and belief among the laity, summarized by the mayor of Barcelona: "The old-fashioned idea is faith, heaven, and God. The new idea is science, earth and man."[2]

1. My translation. Statutes, or primitive legislation, of the new institute were written and approved in 1880.

2. Yañez, *Hemos Creido en el Amor,* 80 (my translation).

Raphaela was born into a world of inequalities. She lived in a society inhabited by the rich and the poor. Her own family was wealthy landed gentry who owned all the land and properties in the area and an estate in Cordoba. But she inherited a special love for the poor from her father, Don Ildefonso Porras, the mayor of Pedro Abad, a love uncommon among the local aristocracy of those times. In Raphaela's biography we read that Don Ildefonso, who had an unusual social awareness and sense of justice, allowed the "small tenant farmers of Pedro Abad and the surrounding villages, to profit from his large warehouse." He also had an "unusual credit system of almost unlimited, interest free loans," and, the biographer recounts, "if someone died without paying off his debts, Don Ildefonso would cancel them immediately for the widow and her children."[3] The solidarity of Don Ildefonso with the poor reached its heroic limit during a cholera epidemic in the town. He chose not to leave with the other wealthy landowners, but stayed to look after the sick. He purchased medicines for them, organized the funerals of those who died, and eventually, succumbed to the sickness himself. He gave his own life for his people.

Raphaela inherited the same caring concern for the poor and needy from her mother, Doña Rafaela, also. It was at her side that Raphaela met with poverty and pain for the first time, visiting the poor and sick of the village. She got to know the poor farmers of Pedro Abad all by name, recognizing each face, and counted them among her friends.

But above all, Raphaela was also familiar with the Bible, which for a woman was unheard of at the time. She read the Word of God regularly and prayerfully. In its pages, she had met and come to know the God of the Hebrew Scriptures: the Liberator of his people, the Protector of the Poor. She encountered the God who hears the cry of his people and knows their need. She learned of the God of the orphan, the widow, and the stranger, who speaks the language of human rights and asks of us that we too "act justly, love tenderly and walk humbly with our God."[4] She came across

---

3. Yañez, *Hemos Creido en el Amor*, 80 (my translation).
4. Mic 6:8.

the God of Life who defends the lives of those who are the most vulnerable, the most threatened, and the most trampled.

Raphaela was also a woman who had fallen passionately in love with Jesus Christ: the Christ of the gospel who came to "announce the good news to the poor, to proclaim liberty to captives, sight to the blind, to set the downtrodden free . . ."[5] She loved the poor and humble Christ who by healing the sick and by associating with women and with "sinners" returned their dignity to them. She was committed to Christ, whose special friends and table companions were the poor and marginalized. These were Raphaela's special friends too, and a friendship which she incarnated in a radical option for the poor.

This heritage came to fruition with the famous decision of Raphaela and her sister Dolores. They said, "We have been served long enough, now it is time for us to serve."[6] It was a decision to dedicate themselves to the service of the sick and the poor of Pedro Abad, as both their father and mother had done. But they took it a step further, renouncing their privileges and sharing in the housework equally with the servants. Curiously, this was a decision made in a Spain where among the liberals, the ideals of liberalism—justice, freedom and equality—were flourishing. It was indeed a revolutionary but gospel-based decision that contravened the criteria and customs of their social class, and one that shocked their close family members, igniting the righteous indignation of their brothers. They particularly disapproved of their sisters tending the sick personally and attempted to thwart their charitable tasks. But the sisters, particularly Raphaela, were extremely creative in finding ways to carry on their work, with the complicity of trusted servants.

I do not think that Raphaela chose explicitly to defend "human rights." She did not learn the vocabulary used in the "Declaration of the rights of man and of the citizen" of 1789. But spontaneously she used the same language. She was a woman of God who had surprising insights and she knew how to incarnate

---

5. Luke 4:18.
6. Yañez, *Cimientos Para un Edificio*, 28.

her biblical spirituality into an option for the poor and human development. At the same time, Raphaela lived in a country in the throes of a liberal revolution, which exalted the ideas of justice and human rights, even though it was also characterized by the anti-religious attitude and violence of the people who proclaimed those very rights. At the same time, Raphaela worshiped in a church in which Leo XIII was to write the first papal encyclical in 1891 on social issues and justice: *Rerum Novarum*. Raphaela, who was interested in "everything that was taking place everywhere,"[7] would have undoubtedly been aware of this social movement in the world and the church.

Their brothers were unrelenting in their opposition of the determination of Raphaela and Dolores to serve the poor. This undoubtedly proved to be the catalyst that facilitated the expression of their independence and precipitated their decision to enter a convent and become religious Sisters. So Raphaela, Dolores, and some of their friends with whom they had shared their dream, left Pedro Abad to begin their journey and to open a new chapter entitled the Handmaids of the Sacred Heart of Jesus.

It was only to be expected that the religious institute founded by Raphaela would share her sensitivity towards the poor, the excluded, and the marginalized from the very beginning. The Handmaids of the Sacred Heart would dedicate themselves to the evangelization of everyone, with a preference given to the poor, particularly poor girls, to whom they would offer "religious and social education completely free."[8] Illiteracy in Spain at the time was rated at 75 percent to 63 percent and was highest among women in rural areas. The Sisters' aim was to educate them out of poverty and in this way change society.

The beginnings of the institute were not easy for the foundresses and their companions. The first phase of their journey was characterized by uncertainty and daring leaps of faith. Initially the group of young women, with the approval of the local bishop, entered the institute of Marie Reparatrice in 1875 as novices with

---

7. Yañez, *Cimientos Para un Edificio*, 28.
8. Yañez, *Hemos Creido en el Amor*, 10 (my translation).

a view to opening a school in Cordoba. However, this project was short-lived. While Raphaela and the others learned the practices of institutional religious life and joyfully imbibed the Ignatian spirituality and eucharistic spirit of the Sisters, the bishop and the "French nuns" failed to agree on the projected educational ministry and, after a series of complications and misunderstandings, the Reparatrice Sisters left Cordoba for Seville, taking four of the Spanish novices with them. Raphaela and the other fifteen novices elected to remain there with the bishop's blessing and under his authority, and thus fulfill their original intention: "the salvation and social regeneration of the diocese."[9]

For a short time, all seemed well. The bishop was happy and the young novices, with Raphaela appointed as Superior, continued living their religious life in preparation for their first vows. They were totally unaware of the adventure that awaited them. The bishop, who was a member of the Dominican Order, decided to introduce changes into the way of life that they were about to profess: no more Ignatian spirituality, reduced hours of eucharistic adoration, and a strict enclosure, together with an ultimatum of twenty-four hours to accept his proposals. But the novices wanted the rules of St. Ignatius and to maintain the eucharistic dimension of their life that defined their identity and their vocation. They felt that taking these away from them was tantamount to tearing the core of their being out of their lives: who they were and who God wanted them to be. They were all in total agreement: "We will not make our vows like this."[10] Instead, they decided to leave Cordoba by night, and set out on a journey to find a bishop who would allow them to live the life to which they felt called. Their first stop was Andujar, a neighboring town, and from there they made their way to Madrid, where Cardinal Moreno, Archbishop of Toledo and Primate of Spain, gave them permission to establish a religious community in the Spanish Capital on April 14, 1877. The congregation of the Handmaids of the Sacred Heart of Jesus was finally born and joined the ranks of the many new institutes that

---

9. Yañez, *Hemos Creido en el Amor*, 11 (my translation).
10. Yañez, *Cimientos Para un Edificio*, 56 (my translation).

were founded in Europe in the nineteenth century. The majority of them, like the Handmaids, were dedicated to the alleviation of the material and spiritual misery of their time, in a concerted effort to rebuild the world.

The small group of young women set themselves up in a tiny apartment, where they initiated their new congregation's double mission of prayer and ministry, of public worship of the Blessed Sacrament, and the apostolic activity of education. Both of these were permeated by a spirit of reparation.[11] Burning with love for Christ in the Eucharist and the "concern that devoured his Heart" for the salvation of mankind, they began crafting the statutes of the congregation, the first written legislation of the order, which summarized the identity and basic aims of the institute:

> ... in order to respond to this immense love of Jesus Christ we shall dedicate our life to adoring him in the Eucharist and to work so that everyone may know and love him ... we shall teach doctrine, especially to poor children, but also to others who need it ... we shall receive into our houses persons who wish to make the spiritual exercises and, any other pious works that may be deemed necessary in the future.[12]

And that is precisely what they did.

Meanwhile, the congregation grew and expanded. Many young women joined them and they founded communities and schools in other cities in Spain: Cordoba,[13] Jerez de la Frontera, Zaragoza, and Bilbao. But there were still years of work ahead: the formation and care of the growing membership and young and inexperienced Superiors, the accompaniment of new communities, new needs in society to be addressed, and the development

---

11. Reparation was understood at that time by the Sisters as "redressing" or "making amends for" the ingratitude of mankind and its frigid response to his immense love for us.

12. Yanez, *Hemos Creido en el Amor*, 11–13 (my translation).

13. The Handmaids' first new foundation was in Cordoba, where they returned to the open arms of the bishop. All was forgiven!

of the mission. Wanting to be "universal like the church,"[14] the Handmaids began to reach out beyond Spain, and sought papal approbation. At the same time, constitutions had to be written, corrected, and submitted. Both Raphaela and Dolores were directly involved in this work, particularly in the chapter that explicitly identified the mission of the Handmaids.

But many internal and external vicissitudes buffeted the Handmaids in those early years. An episcopal tussle with the bishop of Madrid proved time consuming and very frustrating. Sickness and the deaths of some of the young Sisters from tuberculosis was disheartening. But above all, misunderstandings and conflict within the general government forced Raphaela to resign as Superior General in 1892. Later Dolores, who had replaced her sister, was deposed in 1903. But although both of them were relegated to relative and separate obscurity until they died—Dolores in 1916 and Raphaela in 1925—the Institute, whose foundation stones they were, continued to flourish and develop. And the seeds of the mission that they had sown put down roots and grew steadily for many years in the lives of the Handmaids of the Sacred Heart all over the world.

Then Vatican Council II occurred, calling for a renewal of the Catholic Church, for a compassionate dialogue with contemporary society, for peace, and for social justice. The council also urged the renewal of religious communities as members of the church, inviting them to return to their biblical roots and their founding charisms, and to develop a greater outreach to and dialogue with the modern world. For the Handmaids, this meant reigniting their passion for Jesus Christ in the gospel and the Eucharist and recapturing the founding spirit and dream of Raphaela, Dolores, and the first Sisters. Consequently, they felt called to engage more radically with the people whom they served, seeking out new methods of ministry more relevant to the current times.

---

14. Raphaela expressed this desire in 1886 to Mgr. Della Chiesa, the then secretary to the Papal Nuncio and the future Pope Benedict XV.

In response to Vatican II, the Handmaids convoked a special General Congregation[15] in 1969 to plan for and to chart the renewal and adaptation of the Institute. In GC XI[16] the sisters reclaimed their heritage:

> In these moments of adequate renovation in which the Church asks us to return to the sources, bearing in mind that our charism can be understood only in the light of the life of our Mother Foundresses, who are the best example of their own work, in whom the mission of the Institute is vitally expressed, the need for all the religious in the Congregation to have a deep knowledge and love of the Mothers whom God gave us as the foundation of the Institute, is more obvious than ever.

They reaffirmed the essential elements that identify the Sisters, that "make the Handmaids, Handmaids," and the reason why they exist: to be gospel women in love with Jesus Christ in the Eucharist, who hear the cry of the poor and whose hearts beat to the rhythm of the heart of Christ as they share in Christ's mission to redeem the world.

> The life of a Handmaid of the Sacred Heart of Jesus is realized fully and dynamically by living the celebration of the Eucharist in depth, by means of sacramental communion and an integral participation in the intention of Christ, who offers himself to the Father for the salvation of his brothers. This attitude of full participation in Christ's redemptive sacrifice is prolonged after Mass by Eucharistic adoration, which is the continuation of sacramental communion with Christ and by apostolic action in the service of our brothers.[17]

They reiterated that

---

15. General Congregations are regular meetings made up of Sisters representing the communities worldwide to elect leadership and/or charter a future course for the Institute. Each General Congregation issues an unpublished report for the Sisters.
16. Handmaids, General Congregation XI, 15.
17. Handmaids, General Congregation XI, 3.

the apostolic action proper to the Institute, already stated in its first documents and lived since its origins is education in faith . . . that includes educational activities which cover all stages of women's formation and is open to all social classes . . . keeping in mind that it is according to the charism of the Institute to give preference to the education of the poor" . . . and centers of spirituality.[18]

They included for the first time in their legislation a section dedicated specifically to their apostolate with the poor, in contemporary language: a section that surely caused Raphaela to jump with joy in heaven:

> The Institute is to continue to give priority to apostolate with the poor, dedicating the greater part of our apostolic activity to those in most need, those who, in working-class areas, slums, rural districts and under-developed countries are crying out for promotion and are begging our help. This is demanded by the spirit of our Mother Foundresses . . . our legislation and the present directives of the Church.[19]

The Handmaids set about translating this renewal into reality, each in their own geopolitical context. The Sisters based in Latin America followed the more progressive stance of the Conference of Latin American Bishops (CELAM), expounded in the Conference of Medellin in 1968, that officially supported base ecclesial communities, and the Liberation Theology initiated by Gustavo Gutiérrez. The Conference in Puebla in 1979 defined the concept of a "preferential option for the poor" very graphically, with a gallery of faces illustrating the suffering of the poor, the needy, the marginalized: "This situation of pervasive extreme poverty takes on very concrete faces in real life. In these faces we ought to recognize the suffering features of Christ our Lord."[20]

---

18. Handmaids, General Congregation XI, 6.
19. Handmaids, General Congregation XI, 124.
20. Document of CELAM Conference, Puebla, 1979. Quoted in *50 Years On: Probing the Riches of Vatican II*, edited by David Schultenover, 332. Collegeville, MN: Liturgical Press, 2015.

Many Sisters worked on acquiring training and a social formation that was both theoretical and practical. At the same time, many communities inserted themselves into the poor areas where they were serving the people in order to be closer to them. They steeped themselves and the students in their schools, from each and every social environment, in the social teaching of the Catholic Church.

The Vatican Council had also mandated the revision of the constitutions of religious communities. Accordingly, the Handmaids initiated a ten-year program of prayer and reflection, evaluation, research, and consultation, involving the participation and co-responsibility of their total membership, to draw up guidelines for rewriting the constitutions as an articulation of the Institute's identity, mission, and life in inspirational and visionary terms. It also included its community structures in a harmonious blend of spiritual and juridical elements. During that process, Raphaela was canonized in 1977, an event that offered the Handmaids a very moving opportunity to value her heritage even more and acknowledge her proudly once again as the living soul of the Institute, both at its foundation and throughout its subsequent history.

The Sisters who attended General Congregation XII in 1977 determined the content to be included in the revised constitutions. Then, during General Congregation XIII in 1982, the Sisters crafted the text of the document. Presenting it to the Institute, they recommended that all the Handmaids "rediscover existentially our charism's powerful force for spreading the Gospel and incarnating it so we can offer it with joy as a response to the needs of today's world."[21]

The revised constitutions did rediscover Raphaela's vision, but expressed it in terms of the new developments in theology and biblical exegesis. Moreover, they were permeated with the Handmaids' passionate love for God's people, contemplated with tenderness through the eyes of women. But just as Raphaela lived her dream in response to the needs of her time, the Handmaids were being challenged to do the same in their world:

21. Handmaids, General Congregation XIII, 23–24.

> Let us make a great effort to bring them alive, with all the riches of personal touches with which God interiorly calls each one of us, and with the diversity of place and circumstance in which each community has to develop the mission of the Institute. Let us all be alive, fruitfully alive, transmitting the life that encourages, the life centered on the Eucharist, which bears witness to the immense love of Jesus Christ—bread and wine in men's hands—and proclaims the coming of the Kingdom. The field of our apostolate is immense; there is much poverty in the world, much injustice, much suffering, many men and women still unevangelized. All of this urges us to give ourselves without reserve; the Constitutions show us how to do it in Raphaela's way.[22]

That has been the challenge of the Handmaids ever since. As the Institute continued to grow in numbers and extend its outreach to other countries and different ministries, particularly with and for the poor and marginalized. They continued to celebrate General Congregations, to elect leadership, and to ensure the ongoing renewal of the vitality and spirit of the Institute, allowing the changing needs of the times and the development of theology to challenge their creativity. Each gathering deepened the Sisters' sense of their identity and, gradually, developed their understanding of their mission.

General Congregation XIV provided pastoral guidelines for the Sisters' ministry, marked by their shared vision and identity. Solidarity with suffering humanity and the option for the poor were seen as the touchstone for all their pastoral ministry:

> The recent foundations made among the poor have helped us to live in a more real way our option for the most needy, to be more consistent in our promotion of justice in love and to make this option effective no matter where we are working. At the same time the experience certain communities have of being inserted in poor neighborhoods has given us the means of acquiring a

---

22. Hernaez, Ana Maria. Correspondence to the Handmaids of the Sacred Heart of Jesus (April 3, 1983).

more existential knowledge of social injustice as it exists today and a better understanding of the demands of our charism of reparation.[23]

This experience needed to overflow into all the Handmaids' ministries: "It seems urgent for us to concretize our promotion of justice in existential forms that will motivate us and encourage those with whom we work to be agents of social change in the situations in which we are living." The Handmaids' commitment to social justice now had a new dimension; they wanted to help to build a "new society that is just and caring."[24]

The Institute took yet another new step in its commitment to social justice in 1992. Following Pope John Paul's encyclical *Sollicitudo Rei Socialis* in 1987 that had introduced a new term —"social sin" and "structures of sin"—into the vocabulary of the Church's teaching on social justice, the Handmaids, in their General Congregation XV, for the first time denounced structural injustice in their role as "breach-menders" in a world of contrasts: life and death, peace and violence, solidarity and discrimination. They testified that they had heard the cry of "injustice, insolidarity, lack of sensitivity in the face of structural sin, and the destruction of natural resources, which give rise to misery, marginalization, and an anti-culture of violence and death in our world."[25]

In practical terms, this meant that the Sisters did their best to be even closer to the poor and marginalized, more incarnated in their reality, allowing the Sisters to be evangelized by them. They recommitted themselves to work for justice wherever they lived and ministered, taking very seriously the call of the Church and the Congregation to denounce structural sin. The Sisters in Latin America took the lead, some of them working side by side on a voluntary basis with women working long hours for low pay as temporary *obreras* (workers) on farms, in order to denounce the system and to defend the women's rights. The Sisters in Ecuador began living among the indigenous peoples and standing

23. Handmaids, General Congregation XIV, 23.
24. Handmaids, General Congregation XIV, 27.
25. Handmaids, General Congregation XV, 34.

with them, sometimes at personal risk to themselves. The Sisters in India opened a community among the despised tribal people, while in Vietnam they opened a "Love School" for street kids and a kindergarten for abandoned orphans in Africa.

Looking forward to the third millenium, in General Congregation XVI, the Handmaids recognized that they had moved closer to the world of the poor in every country where they lived and worked, but they expressed a desire to be yet more sensitive to the emptiness of humanity and its sorrow, from a more compassionate heart and in greater solidarity, opting always for the weakest and the smallest. They proposed opening a dialogue of life and work with those trying to make the world more just and humane, such as other ecclesial organizations, institutions, and groups from other confessions and beliefs. The way forward in the fight for social justice was now along the path of communion and collaboration.[26] This marked a new initiative for the Handmaids, who until then had worked intensely as protagonists in many fields of ministry in a global context. They now needed to push the boundaries of their own great spirit of communion in their diversity to embrace others who care deeply and struggle to protect the rights of each and every person. They also took the collaborative step that some other religious congregations had already taken, some of them a long time ago, by opening their arms to embrace all those who wished to share their mission and Raphaela's spirit by creating the international "ACI Family" (named for the Latin initials of the Handmaids, *Ancilla Cordis Iesu*).

The Handmaids celebrated General Congregation XVII in 2002, in response to Pope John Paul II's apostolic letter *Novo Millennio Ineunte*, with its future oriented theme: "Put out into the deep." The Sisters, who had lived intensely the Jubilee Year that inaugurated the new millenium and also the 150th anniversary of the birth of St. Raphaela, now found themselves on the 125th anniversary of the birth of the Institute facing new horizons with a wider sense of communion and universality, as consecrated women in the world and for the world.

26. Handmaids, General Congregation XVI, 1997.

Looking back, the Handmaids recognized that in the preceding years they had attempted to give "multiple responses to new forms of poverty, causing a change of standpoint in our work with the poor. We had turned little by little from going towards the poor, to standing alongside them and working with them." Those new forms of poverty had included immigrants, those displaced by violence, the homeless, those who lacked food, health, or education, indigenous people, and prisoners. The Handmaids had experienced that their passion for Christ had deepened their passion for the suffering of the world. The call now was to contemplate the world from the Heart of Christ, a globalized world that was rocked by an explosion of violence, by open warfare in various countries and by growing violence in society and the family, and to enter into a dialogue between that world and the Handmaids' charism. In this dialogue, the Sisters, as women called to build a culture of peace and reconciliation, would renew their commitment to solidarity and to raising awareness of all forms of injustice. Above all, they decided on a new option: to promote the dignity of women, especially women who have been exploited and impoverished and are in need of integral development. This option is what would permeate the Handmaids' life and work during the coming years.

Those years, 2002–2007, enjoyed a distinctly eucharistic climate, punctuated with a series of eucharistic events. In 2003 Pope John Paul II published his encyclical *Ecclesia de Eucharistia*, "to rekindle this Eucharistic 'amazement.'"[27] The following year, he issued an apostolic letter entitled *Mane Nobiscum Domine* ("Stay with us, Lord"), announcing an International Eucharistic Congress to be held in Guadalajara, Mexico (October 2004) and designating 2005 as the Year of the Eucharist. The year would close with the eleventh Synod of Bishops with the theme: "The Eucharist Source and Summit of the Life and Mission of the Church." Finally, at the beginning of 2007, Benedict XVI issued a post-synodal apostolic exhortation, *Sacramentum Caritatis* ("Sacrament of Charity"),

27. John Paul II, *Ecclesia de Eucharistia*, 6. http://www.vatican.va/holy_father/special_features/encyclicals/documents/hf_jp-ii_enc_20030417_ecclesia_eucharistia_en.html.

highlighting the social implications of the Eucharist. These were years that provided an opportunity for the Handmaids to reflect on and reimagine Eucharist in its full extension,[28] and to rediscover in the Eucharist a theological basis for the social doctrine of the Catholic Church.

These were also years that witnessed a growing consensus worldwide about the alleviation of poverty. In UK, the Make Poverty History Campaign wanted 2005 remembered as the "year that changed the world." Rock stars and music groups attempted to raise public awareness about poverty in Africa with a series of Live 8 concerts, playing and singing for "political justice." In 2006, *TIME* magazine named its "Persons of the Year": Bill and Melinda Gates and Bono, describing them as "three people on a global mission to end poverty, disease and indifference."[29] That year the Academy Awards all went to movies that focused on social issues: homosexuality, racism, corruption, and corporate crime.

Against the background of this eucharistic and social ferment so close to their hearts, the Handmaids celebrated General Congregation XVIII in 2007. Using a eucharistic framework to express their insights, the Sisters recalled once again that the Eucharist, in its totality, celebrated, adored, and lived was the experience that aroused in Raphaela an apostolic spirit with a universal outreach. Determined to be bread broken and wine poured out for others, they focused on the effects of migration and illiteracy that widen the poverty cycle and, in turn, degrade the dignity of people. "We hear the call to work with greater determination to restore to our brothers and sisters affected by these situations that dignity that is theirs by right and to do even more to break the poverty cycle."[30] To accomplish this, they opted to do so in dialogue, in collaboration, and by networking with others.

28. The Handmaids' understanding of the Eucharist had now developed beyond celebration and adoration to include living eucharistic attitudes and being Eucharist.

29. Gibbs, Nancy. "The Good Samaritans: Melinda Gates, Bono and Bill Gates: three people on a global mission to end poverty, disease—and indifference." *Time* 166.26 (December 26, 2005).

30. Handmaids, General Congregation XVIII, 2007.

The spirit and practice of networking that had been developing gradually among the Handmaids, particularly in their commitment to social justice and the service of the poor, was revisited by General Congregation XIX in 2012, where it was given a completely new focus and expression. Energized by their charism that was being continually rekindled by the world and its pain, the Handmaids now wanted to allow that charism to become a burning passion in their lives: a passion that overflows into a compassionate embrace, reaching out to all the suffering and nurturing life, a driving, urgent passion that confirmed that the poor and the earth could not wait any longer. At the same time, painfully aware of their own complicity in social injustice and the destruction of creation, they restated their commitment to take a stance in response to the cry of the impoverished, especially women and children who are victims of human trafficking, and to the whimper of the wounded earth: two cries that come together in a single heart-rending groan.[31] But the stand that was needed now was one that involved not only working to alleviate the effects of injustice on the ground, but also fighting for the systemic change of unjust structures that underlie the inequalities that engender poverty. It was time to challenge the oppressive systems that undermine the dignity and human rights of so many men, women, and children in our world. And what more appropriate place to make that stand than at the United Nations, whose core purpose is the respect for and protection of human rights? And what better way to proceed than by joining the ranks of the NGOs to be a voice for human rights, justice, and the integrity of creation within the halls of the meeting place of the whole international community?

Realizing that their Institute was too small, with insufficient resources to become an NGO in its own right, the Handmaids opted to join a coalition of smaller religious congregations that already enjoyed consultative status at the UN.

The Handmaids of the USA Province had already investigated possible options in New York and shared their findings with the Sisters gathered in Rome. Hence, despite the misgivings of some

---

31. Handmaids, General Congregation XIX, 2012.

Sisters who saw many flaws in the practices of the United Nations Organization, General Congregation XIX made a formal commitment to apply for membership of UNANIMA International in order to become gospel women at the UN, supporting exploited women and children and to care for the earth more effectively. Their application was accepted and the Handmaids became full members of UNANIMA in 2012.

Raphaela's heritage of love for the poor and vulnerable, developed gradually over time in her Congregation, the Handmaids of the Sacred Heart, and kept pace with the expansion of the Institute, the growth of the social teaching of the Church and theological investigation, and, above all, the explosive spread of poverty all over the globe. Raphaela died before the UN was founded, but her horizons had always been very broad, and she carried within her heart "millions and millions" of people. Always daring and even subversive in finding ways to serve the poor, she surely walks the corridors of the UN, side by side with the members of UNANIMA there, exclaiming, "How many children God has!"

Chapter 6

UNANIMA International and Its Aims

BUT WHO AND WHAT is UNANIMA International that wrote the Handmaids into their story in 2012? And when and how did their narrative begin?

UNANIMA International (UI) was an initiative of and for the new millennium. It also added one more name to the long list of religious women who, as protagonists of gospel-based concern for the weakest and the least, have committed their lives to standing with the poor and to taking their cause to the public square. UI began at the 2002 meeting of the Leadership Conference of Women Religious in the United States (LCWR), when Sr. Catherine Ferguson, a Sister of the Holy Names of Jesus and Mary, invited any womens' religious congregations with a strong commitment to justice and interest in becoming more active in shaping global policy to form a coalition RNGO to advocate at the United Nations on behalf of women and children.

Six months later, Catherine received ten responses from interested religious congregations. In December 2001, representatives of seven[1] congregations met to inaugurate the coalition and

---

1. Carmelite Sisters of Charity (Vedruna), Congregation of the Sisters of

UNANIMA INTERNATIONAL AND ITS AIMS

to develop a mission statement, a timeline, a budget, and a name. UNANIMA International (UI) had been born. The name is significant. It begins with "UN" for the United Nations, while "ANIMA" is Latin for feminine "spirit," indicating a desire to bring a feminine spirit to the UN. As its name also indicates, UI is a group acting with one heart and one mind. The founding members also crafted a shared mission statement:

> UNANIMA International is a coalition of congregations of women religious with members on all continents, committed to work for peace and human dignity in response to the needs of our world by service to our members, to the United Nations, to other NGOs through collaboration, education and action in affiliation with the UN regarding: Women and children, particularly the economically poor, immigrants and refugees, and the welfare of the planet.[2]

June 2002 marked the official corporate beginning of UI as a nonprofit organization incorporated in the state of New York with a board of directors. Each of the congregations of women religious who were members of UI was required to nominate a representative on the board for a three-year term and also a liaison person between the leadership of each congregation and UI.[3] At the first board meeting in September 2002, the bylaws were accepted and each congregation was asked to commit to a three-year membership. The UI board appointed Sr. Catherine Ferguson to be the UI coordinator and chose as its special area of focus and action for the next two years, violence against women through the trafficking of women and children. Within the context of the United Nations, they committed themselves to work for the prevention of traffick-

---

St. Agnes, Missionary Sisters of the Sacred Heart of Jesus (Cabrini), Religious of Jesus and Mary, Sisters of the Holy Names of Jesus and Mary, Society of the Holy Child Jesus, and Ursuline Sisters of Mount St. Joseph—numbering 7,200 Sisters and associates in all continents.

2. UNANIMA, "Board Members' Handbook," 1.

3. This structure was meant to ensure a two-way communication system between UNANIMA and the member congregations, with both their leadership and the grassroots.

ing and to promote alternatives for those who were at risk of being trafficked.

UNANIMA International now had an identity and a mission. But it lacked a forum. The next task to be addressed was gaining access to the United Nations. By the fall of 2004, UNANIMA International was accepted for UN Department of Public Information (DPI) status, and in 2005 was granted special consultative status with the UN Economic and Social Council (ECOSOC). Now an accredited NGO, UI found the door open for Sr. Catherine and her small staff to navigate the complex aeropagus that is the UN with its maze of corridors and departments, covering a myriad of issues in order to initiate their mission.

They immediately became involved with the United Nations Committee to Eliminate all forms of Discrimination against Women (CEDAW), making interventions at CEDAW sessions and developing action plans. UI also participated in UN NGO working groups in social development, the eradication of poverty, HIV/AIDS, girls, children's rights, and the Permanent Forum on Indigenous Peoples UI joined the planning group for the Commission on the Status of Women and the Coalition against Trafficking of Women (CATW). By this time, UI had a membership of 12 religious congregations, numbering 15,700 Sisters located in 61 countries.[4]

From the beginning, UI had also initiated an internship program for Sisters of member congregations in order to provide them with an educational experience of working at the UN. Interns would join the UNANIMA staff for about three months, to learn about the structure of the United Nations and the NGOs and RNGOs within it. In this way, they would learn lobbying skills and be provided with an opportunity to work for systemic change and better policies in the UI focus areas. They would be encouraged to research social justice issues in their own areas of expertise and attend sessions of NGO Committees working on those issues. The

---

4. To the original seven members the following congregations were added: Brigidine Sisters, Sisters of the Holy Union, Sisters of Providence, Congregation of Bons Secours, and the Sisters of St. Anne.

first UI intern was Sr. Ana Martinez de Lucco, a Vedruna Sister. At the same time, UI also offered an alternative immersion program for Sisters who could only dedicate a short period of time to working at the UN.

In 2006, UNANIMA International refined its focus on trafficking to address the demand for women and children trafficked for sexual exploitation. It designed a "Stop the Demand" campaign which was launched the following year. Simultaneously, the board decided to create a Woman of Courage Award, to be granted annually to a woman who embodied in her life the values and principles of the UN, whose actions related to one of the major areas of concern of UI and who had displayed commitment and courage in the face of adversity or intimidation. The first annual Woman of Courage Award, in 2008, honored Lydia Cacho Ribeiro, a journalist and women's rights activist from Mexico who had founded a shelter and crisis center for victims of sex-crimes, gender-based violence, and human trafficking.

In the following years, UNANIMA International continued to extend its work at the UN and to adjust its focus as new priorities presented themselves. It also regularly welcomed new members. In 2009, as a response to the Earth Charter,[5] UI chose to focus its environmental advocacy over the following three years on "Water as a Right," providing leadership in the promotion and recognition of water as a common good to be preserved for use by all life-forms on the planet. In 2011, Sr. Catherine Ferguson resigned as UI Coordinator and Sr. Michele Morek, an Ursuline Sister, was appointed as her successor. The following year, Sr. Michele together with Sr. Kathleen Ries, UI Board President, attended the Rio+20 United Nations Conference on Sustainable Development in Rio de Janeiro,[6] bringing back a very excited and detailed report

---

5. The Earth Charter or the Peoples Treaty was created by NGOs and indigenous peoples throughout the world. It sought to inspire a sense of global interdependence and responsibility for the care of the planet.

6. Rio20+ issued a final document, "The Future We Want," that called for corporate sustainable development. It laid the groundwork for the 8 Millenium Development Goals, (MDGs) to be replaced by 17 Sustainable Development Goals (SGDs). See: https://sustainable development.un.org/rio20.html.

on the high and low points of the conference to the next board meeting. At that meeting, the directors engaged in a long-range planning process, from which the overarching focus of climate change emerged. They also affirmed an addendum to the UI mission statement to reflect that shift in emphasis:

> The reality of climate change and its devastating effects heightens our need to reexamine its impact on the vulnerable. Our mission impels us to respond to Rio+20's call for sustainable development and engage the grassroots with the UN to work on the global crisis that threatens the quality of life for all.[7]

Two years later, true to that mission, Sr. Michele, the UI President and a staff member, were among the thousands of delegates who attended the historic UNFCC Climate Conference in Paris (COP 21) where 195 countries reached a landmark accord that, for the first time, committed nearly every country in the world to lowering planet-warming carbon emissions.

In UI's work for sustainable development, mining and fracking were seen as two issues of major concern to its members. At this time, UI became very instrumental in the revitalization of the Mining Working Group (MWG) at the UN with its rights-based approach to sustainable development. As a result, UI staff and members became very active in advocating for human and environmental rights being threatened by the unjust and unsustainable practices and policies of extractive industries. The urgency of this situation was intensified by data being provided by UI members who had Sisters working with local communities in South America, especially with indigenous peoples, whose lives and livelihood were being held hostage to the interests of foreign mining companies, often with the complicity of local governments. So much so that, in 2015, the UI board decided to give its Woman of Courage Award to Maxima Acuna de Chaupe, a courageous Peruvian peasant farmer, who was defending her life, her family, her little hut, and her tiny plot of land, all of which were being threatened by the

---

7. UNANIMA, "Board Members' Handbook," 4.

extraction project of a huge gold-mining company. When she testified to human rights officials in Paris, Belgium, and Geneva, men from the company beat her and her husband, killed their livestock, and threatened their lives. Members of UNANIMA International working in Peru with indigenous people, knew Maxima and were supporting her in her struggle. Simultaneously, the UI staff took her case to the UN through the MWG in order to try to guarantee her protection.

As well as acting as a member of various UN committees and NGO coalitions, UI also developed its networking outreach to other organizations. UI was already a member of the International Catholic Organization (ICO), the Interfaith Committee for Religious NGOs, and Religious at the UN (RUN), but its commitment to working in partnership went beyond the bounds of the UN. In 2013, Sr. Michele attended the "charter meeting" as a founding member of US Catholic Sisters Against Human Trafficking (USCSAHT). This meeting was followed by a visit to the White House to meet with the president's advisory council on faith-based partnerships for the launch of the document on trafficking entitled: "Building Partnerships to Eradicate Modern Day Slavery." UI also made significant contributions across global networks, becoming a parallel organization with Australian Catholic Religious Against Trafficking in Humans (APWRATH), Comité D'Action Contre La Traite Humaine Interne et Internationale (CATHII) in Canada, and the Asian Pacific Women Religious Against Trafficking in Humans (APWRATH). UI is also associated with Talitha Kum, an international organization of religious women against trafficking, sponsored by the Union of Superiors General in Rome (USIG).

During these years greater importance was also given to interaction between UNANIMA International and the Sisters working at the grassroots and to regional collaboration between member congregations of the coalition. Sr. Catherine had travelled to Kenya in 2010, where she visited grassroots projects and presented a workshop on human trafficking focused on "youth teaching youth." This developed into a two-year program, training Catholic young people to train others in parishes in Nairobi how to recognize and combat human trafficking. Three years later, UI also sponsored a two-day workshop—coordinated by board member, Sr. Cecilia Nya, SHCJ—in Ghana for clerics and laypeople working against trafficking in eight countries in East Africa. By networking and producing resource material, UI has tried to provide members with tools to work on issues of concern in their own countries at both regional and local levels. It has also facilitated a network project to connect UI Sisters with each other to share resources and common concerns.

It was during these same years that the Handmaids of the Sacred Heart of Jesus living in the United States decided to investigate the possibility of becoming an NGO at the UN, as a new global way to serve the poor by lobbying for systemic change. In 2011, their inquiries discovered UNANIMA International, a coalition for smaller women's congregations. Two Handmaids, Sr. Sagrario Nunez and Sr. Margaret Scott, made an appointment to visit UI in New York to find out more. There, Sr. Michele Morek introduced them to the UI staff and explained the work they were involved in at the UN. She also detailed the criteria for membership of UI and how to apply. UNANIMA International seemed to be exactly what the Handmaids were looking for. Accordingly, Sr. Michele was invited to address a gathering of all the Sisters of the USA Province of the Handmaids to tell them about UI and to answer their questions. The Handmaids present voted unanimously to apply for membership and tabled a proposal for the next General Congregation to be held in the Spring of 2012, that the Handmaids as an international Congregation apply for membership of UI. In the event that the proposal was not accepted, the Handmaids of the USA Province would proceed to apply for membership just for the Sisters in the US. The General Congregation accepted the motion. Sr. Margaret Scott was asked to present the Handmaids' application at the UI board meeting in September 2012. The application was successful and the Handmaids were accepted as members of UNANIMA International. Sr. Margaret Scott joined the board of Directors and attended her first board meeting in the spring of 2013.

UNANIMA INTERNATIONAL AND ITS AIMS

UI has continued to grow and develop. It now consists of 21 congregations of women religious whose 22,000 members work in 82 countries. Its mission statement, that has evolved in response to the changing needs of international society, now reads:

> UNANIMA International is a non-governmental organization (NGO) advocating on behalf of women and children (particularly those living in poverty and/or who are victims of human trafficking), immigrants and refugees, and the environment and welfare of our planet (particularly issues involving water and climate change).
>
> We are a coalition of communities of religious women who bring their voices, concerns, and experiences as educators, health care providers, social workers, development and community builders to the United Nations. We are committed to working for peace and human dignity in response to the needs of our world, by service to our members, to the United Nations, and to other NGOs and community based groups through advocacy, collaboration, education and action. In our work at the United Nations in New York, we and similar faith-based NGOs aim to educate and influence policymakers at the global level. In solidarity, we work to challenge and change unjust systems at all political levels to achieve a more just world.[8]

The board of directors has become larger and more diverse with the increase of member congregations. We are now a truly international, multicultural group with Sisters from Africa, Australia, Brazil, Canada, Ireland, Spain, the UK, and the US. Our twice-yearly meetings are extremely lively and energizing, as each one shares her "flashpoints": the ideas and actions of her own congregation that conspire to improve the lives of the poor worldwide. We receive updates on UI engagement with UN agencies since the last meeting, and plot and plan our stance on current issues. We also attend UN functions while in New York for board meetings. The spring board meeting is always scheduled to coincide with the UN Commission on the Status of Women's annual two-week

---

8. UNANIMA, "Board Members' Handbook," 1.

conference, enabling us to participate in the many activities, events, meetings, and marches that are organized.

The UI Coordinator and staff spend every day and, at times, every night lobbying at the UN by attending UN meetings and by working on a variety of NGO committees, where they serve as chairs, vice-chairs, secretaries, executive members, and program committee members. They are currently actively involved with:

- NGO Committee for Social Development
- NGO Committee to Stop Trafficking in Persons'
- NGO on Financing for Development
- NGO Committee on Migration
- NGO Civil Society Forum Planning Committee
- Mining Working Group
- Working Group for Girls
- Committee on Integrity of Creation
- NGO Committee on Indigenous People
- NGO Committee on Disarmament

UI also takes issues to the UN by offering its own written and oral interventions to UN working bodies, sometimes during debates. It also engages in direct conversation with the representatives of individual UN member countries and departments. It provides educational papers and side events on different issues during UN conferences that bring its member congregations' grassroots knowledge and experience to the UN. It also provides its membership with tools to work with UN agencies in their own countries.

UI has also invested in social media. After a trial and error period, they now maintain a dynamic, regularly updated website in four languages—English, French, Portuguese, and Spanish[9]—and they have a frequently visited Facebook account.[10] In addition to information about UNANIMA International, the webpage

9. UNANIMA's website: https://www.unanima-international.org.
10. UNANIMA Facebook page: https://www.facebook.com/unanimaint.

includes a great deal of educational material that UI staff and interns have produced on human trafficking and water, mining and climate change, immigration and refugees, social development, and indigenous issues. It incorporates regular updates and also publishes UI's own monthly e-newsletter with the latest news from the UN and from all the member communities around the world.

Recently, UNANIMA International has designed several PowerPoint presentations in different languages for young adults and children that Sisters of member congregations can use in their schools and colleges to raise awareness of UNANIMA International's mission at the United Nations and to encourage their participation in its programs and campaigns. The latest presentation for younger children is particularly simple, yet succinct and informative:

WHAT IS UNANIMA?

We are 22,200 sisters (nuns) who are making the world a better place. Our sisters work in more than 80 countries all over the world.

WHERE ARE WE?

Our office is in New York. We work at the United Nations. But our UNANIMA sisters work all over the world.

WHAT ARE THE SISTERS DOING AT THE UNITED NATIONS?

We remind the UN about the needs of people all over the world.

HOW DO WE DO THAT?

We hold signs! We work to help women and children, especially if they live in poverty, or if they are sold as slaves, or if they have to leave home, or they need good water to drink, or if they need good health or toilets! We want to stop climate change. That means we don't want too many floods, or not enough water, or the world to be too hot, or to have bad storms.

HOW CAN WE DO ALL THIS?

Sometimes we talk in UN Meetings. Sometimes we write papers. Sometimes we work with others. We teach interns so that they can go back to their country and share. We give justice awards to brave women. We hold events at the UN and in other countries. We go to UN meetings, like the Climate Change Meeting in Paris. And we protest for Climate, migrant workers, women . . . And we teach people about the rights of indigenous people, and their lands and water, and, especially about the effects of mining.

And everything we do is included in the UN Sustainable Development Goals, which means that we want to make every person's life better, and that it will last for all the years to come.

That, in a nutshell, is UNANIMA International. But what of the future? What are the challenges that now face both UNANIMA International and the Handmaids of the Sacred Heart of Jesus, as members of UI, in a rapidly changing world?

Conclusion

Handmaids and the UN
Future Challenges for Public Theology

RAPID CHANGE IS GAINING momentum everywhere. Inevitably, the winds of change are bringing unfolding geo-political shifts that are buffeting our global society, and have—and will continue to have—serious consequences for the United Nations. Those consequences will inevitably affect UNANIMA International and also the Handmaids of the Sacred Heart of Jesus in their ongoing commitment to be present in word and action in our world, disfigured as it is by so much human misery and suffering.

In the master narrative of our increasingly turbulent times, the world seems to be in a state of permanent crisis. We see the liberal order being undermined from within and without. Democracy is in decline, rapidly falling into domestic dysfunction. Autocracy, isolationism, and protectionism reign, while a belligerent nationalistic mindset views international institutions and globalization as threats to national sovereignty and security. Rivalry is escalating and power struggles seem potentially unbounded.

While great power rivalry have always been the motor of history, driving events on the global stage, today we are witnessing the same script but with different actors. The breaking news is the rise of China, with all its geopolitical consequences. Clearly, China is threatening the dominance of the United States and economists predict that it will soon have the larger of the two economies. The future will depend, to a large extent, on how Beijing and Washing DC manage their relations. At the same time, China's push towards increased investment in African nations' largely undeveloped infrastructure, particularly mining and oil, is causing concern. That investment represents an enormous increase in China's global political influence and a major growth opportunity for its economy, together with a solid base of raw materials. Of equal concern is the battle for the South China Sea, now dotted with China's artificial and militarized islands.

The second new actor on the global stage is a resurgent Russia. Seen through the lens of the weaponization of cyber and artificial intelligence, its entrance seems to herald the approach of a new cold war between Russia and the West. The "new" Russia under Vladimir Putin has embarked on a systematic challenge to the West, with the apparent goal of weakening the bonds between Europe and the United States and among EU members. It has undertaken a major military modernization to strengthen Russia's strategic position in its immediate neighborhood, and to return Russia to the center of global politics.

But the defining challenge of today, despite the doubts of a few skeptics, is climate change. The disruption of the earth's climate has already begun to seriously influence the global economy and international relations in our warming world. A fascinating example is the Arctic region which is now the site of geopolitical intrigue among the five countries under whose jurisdiction it falls: Canada, Norway, Russia, Denmark, and the US. The Arctic ice is decreasing and thinning, allowing easier access to the oil and gas resources below the sea bed. Russia, to the consternation of the other countries, is intensifying research in the Arctic seabed for obvious economic reasons, while also extending its military presence along the Arctic coast.

All of these current global crises are challenging, or at least throwing into question, the ongoing relevance of the UN. One example is the escalating crisis in Syria. What began as another Arab Spring uprising against an autocratic ruler, Bashar al-Assad, has mushroomed into a brutal proxy war that has drawn in regional and world powers: Russia and Iran, the US, the UK, France, Turkey, Saudi Arabia, Qatar, Jordan, and Israel, each with their own agenda. Meanwhile, after seven years of conflict, the casualties now number at last half a million dead and more than nine million refugees, forcibly displaced from their homes. The crisis is compounded by accusations of the illegal use of chemical weapons and the unspeakable humanitarian tragedy of death, destruction, and misery delivered by bombings, starvation, and sieges.

Where is the United Nations in this situation, committed as it is to brokering peace, protecting civilians, and bringing humanitarian aid? Statements of concern and condemnation have abounded. But little else. The United Nations has been effectively sidelined.

On December 20, 2016, according to the *New York Times*, "Russia, Iran and Turkey met in Moscow to work towards a political solution to end Syria's nearly six year old war, leaving the United States on the sidelines as the countries sought to drive the conflict in ways that serve their interests. Secretary of State John Kerry was not invited. Nor was the United Nations consulted."[1]

Meanwhile the war in Syria continues and escalates, constantly challenging the relevance of the United Nations. Does the UN still have a role to play in international affairs? Some are doubtful.

> This humanitarian catastrophe, [the Syrian civil war] illumines in a palpable way the inadequacies of the present international order. Despite the mandate of the United Nations to prevent war and a range of agreements pledging to protect civilian life, our international institutions have been slow to respond to this humanitarian disaster.[2]

1. Hubbard, Ben. "Russia, Iran and Turkey Meet for Syria Talks, Excluding U.S." *New York Times* (December 20, 2016). https://www.nytimes.com/2016/12/20/world/middleeast/russia-iran-and-turkey-meet-for-syria-talks-excluding-us.html.

2. Ahern, *Public Theology and the Global Common Good*, 14.

"Slow" perhaps, given its complex way of working, but the UN did try and tried hard. It appointed a special envoy to Syria, passed resolutions, albeit non-binding and often unimplemented. It has repeatedly called for an "immediate end to the violence."[3] It has also continually attempted to deliver humanitarian aid, most of which was blocked by the Syrian government. The General Assembly agreed to establish an investigative body to prepare cases on war crimes committed in Syria since 2011. And the UN has pleaded. Stephen O'Brien (OCHA) in a briefing to the Security Council on November 30, 2016 could not have spoken more clearly: "For all the sake of humanity, we call on, we plead, with the parties, and those with influence, to do everything in their power to protect civilians and enable access to the besieged part of eastern Aleppo before it becomes a graveyard."[4] But its pleading has fallen on deaf ears. Its resolutions have often been ignored.

The real reason for the UN's inability to act decisively in the Syrian crisis, as in so many others, has been the Security Council deadlock as a result of the Russian and Chinese vetoes, which have repeatedly been used to obstruct and confuse. Permanent members have focused on scoring political points at home and with their allies rather than building common ground and addressing the war and the human tragedy it is causing. The Security Council is supposed to be able to move swiftly to solve international crises when and where they arise. In the case of the Syrian civil war, it obviously has not been able to do so. In addition to the problem of the permanent members' veto, the situation is further compounded by the fact that four of the permanent members of the Council have been involved militarily in the fighting themselves in various ways. Unfortunately, the UN cannot coerce compliance with its wishes, and the scope of its ability to act is qualified by the interests of the member states, particularly the more powerful among them.

    3. "U.N. Security Council condemns Syrian government crackdown." *CNN* (August 5, 2011). http://www.cnn.com/2011/WORLD/meast/08/03/syria.un/index.html.

    4. "Eastern Aleppo becoming 'one giant graveyard' says UN humanitarian chief." *The Guardian* (November 30, 2016). https://www.theguardian.com/world/2016/nov/30/syria-aleppo-death-toll-united-nations-statistics.

The UN faces other challenges apart from the renewed rivalry among the great powers. It has been dealing with financial difficulties for nearly two decades. "It has been forced to cut back on important programs in all areas, even as new mandates have arisen. Many member states have not paid their full dues and have cut their donations to the UN's voluntary funds."[5] If it is to continue its work, the UN needs a substantial increase in funding. Unfortunately, the UN is no longer a priority for most donor countries. In addition, the UN's financial woes are more and frequently compounded by member states threatening to withhold money unless their interests are safeguarded.[6] In January 2018 the US announced it was withholding $65 million from the UN agency for Palestinian refugees, making future donations contingent on major changes that the US deems necessary in the agency.

The UN is also an aging institution and is in urgent need of reform in its governance and its methods, if it is to adapt to the climate of rising nationalism around the world and growing regional tensions in Asia and the Middle East. That reform needs to begin with the Security Council which no longer reflects the global geo-political reality of the times. The five permanent members represent an imbalance of power, while the 10 rotating seats do not adequately restore regional balance. Asia is particularly underrepresented.[7] Pope Francis underscored the need for reform in his address to the United Nations General Assembly in 2015:

---

5. Global Policy Forum. "UN Finance." https://www.globalpolicy.org/un-finance.html.

6. E.g., in June 2016, Saudi Arabia threatened to withhold hundreds of millions of dollars from UN programs if it was singled out for killing and maiming children. In December 2016, after the Security Council passed a resolution calling for the end of Israeli settlements on Palestinian land, Israel announced that it would cease funding five UN institutions. Members of the US Congress also urged withholding funding for the UN until it reverses its decision. In the case of the US, this is laughable, given that the US regularly defaults on its contributions to the UN!

7. Sachs, Jeffrey. "3 Reforms the UN needs as it turns 70." https://www.weforum.org/agenda/2015/08/3-reforms-the-un-needs-as-it-turns-70/.

The need for greater equity is especially true in the case of those bodies with effective executive capability, such as the Security Council, the Financial Agencies and the groups of mechanisms specifically created to deal with economic crises. This will help limit every kind of abuse or usury, especially where developing countries are concerned.[8]

Addressing these reforms falls to the lot of the new United Nations Secretary General, Antonio Guterres, who was sworn in on December 12, 2016.[9] According to *TIME* magazine:

> He has indicated his first priorities will be to simplify and de-centralize the world's body's sprawling bureaucracy. He is expected to name a female deputy after his appointment disappointed gender-equality campaigners. The on-going civil war in Syria and feisty China also present immediate challenges.[10]

Finally, the United Nations is struggling to survive in a political environment increasingly hostile to multilateral organizations including the UN, the World Bank, IMF, the WTO, and NATO, a political environment in which countries are beginning to question their membership of these organizations and even threatening to leave.[11]

These challenges facing the United Nations will also affect UNANIMA International and its work. UI will, perhaps, have to

---

8. Francis, *Address to the United Nations General Assembly*, 2015. http://w2.vatican.va/content/francesco/en/speeches/2015/september/documents/papa-francesco_20150925_onu-visita.html.

9. The ninth Secretary General is the ex-Prime Minister of Portugal and served as head of the UN Refugee Agency for ten years.

10. John, Tara. "The World's New Diplomat in Chief." *TIME* Magazine (December 26, 2016) 13.

11. CNN reported on August 26th, 2016 that President Duterte of the Philippines had threatened to leave the UN in response to criticism of his approach to drug crimes. President Elect Trump, in one of his now proverbial tweets, announced: "At the UN., things will be different after January 20th!" Now, as president, his "America First" policy is challenging most of these organisations, notably the UN, NATO, and the WTO.

adapt to a different UN, a UN that is reformed or fragmented. But there are other uncertainties that may impact UI. There has been a growing trend in the UN to limit the presence and influence of NGOs. Sr. Michele, in her 2016 report to the board, referred to a growing feeling that NGOs are "irritating" groups to have around. She attributed this to the more noticeable swing to the right in many countries, or perhaps to the composition of the ECOSOC committee on NGOs that is making it increasingly difficult for NGOs to be granted status at the UN.[12] At the same time, NGOs in general are experiencing greater difficulty in being given floor time for oral statements. There are also fewer opportunities for individual NGOs to make interventions unless they are part of a collaborative group like an NGO committee. Many more restrictions are being placed upon UN acceptance of written interventions as well, and the number accepted is tightly controlled. The departure of the US ambassador to the UN, Samantha Power, will also be a great loss to the NGOs at the UN, as hers has always been one of the stronger voices of member states that has defended NGO input on the floor of the Assembly or the Security Council. Her replacement, Nicki Haley, has a less positive relationship with them. She has overseen the resignation of the United States from the UN Human Rights Council, alleging that NGOs were failing to support American-led reform efforts.

UI, together with many other NGOs, was very involved—in partnership with the UN—in the wording of the Sustainable Development Goals (SDGs) that followed Rio+20. But once set, the goals and their targets were placed firmly into the hands of the governments of the members' states to be internally driven. Accordingly, the theater of operations has changed and the focus for lobbying has shifted from the UN itself to individual member countries. UI and its members have now to redirect their energies to the local level.

12. I personally sat through several hours of an ECOSOC committee meeting in which South Africa, China, Russia, and Saudi Arabia consistently rejected applications for NGO status, particularly from organizations of journalists, which they seemed to find particularly annoying.

Lastly, against the background of this new landscape, UN-ANIMA International is also changing. The presidency of the Board of Directors has passed to Sr. Fran Gorsuch of Sisters of Bon Secours, while Sr. Michele has resigned as Coordinator. She has been replaced by Sr. Jean Quinn of Sisters of Divine Wisdom. Sr. Jean, who is Irish, is the first non-American Coordinator of UI. Under this new leadership, UNANIMA is preparing for the unknown future that lies ahead by creating strong and sustainable relationships and by building strong and resilient regional groups wherever we are in the world. It has also has embarked on an evaluation process of who we are, what we do, and why, entitled "A Root and Branch Review." Its purpose is to examine how we can build the organization for a new space and time, and craft a strong, strategic plan for the next five years that will open up new possibilities for UI as it moves forward, given the challenges that face the UN.

As members of UNANIMA International, the Handmaids of the Sacred Heart share those possibilities, just as they have been fully involved in UI work at and through the UN since they joined the coalition. The Handmaids have been present at every board meeting and contributed to the "flashpoints" with reports of the Sisters' work on the ground in several countries. All Handmaids the world over receive the monthly multi-lingual UI briefings and some are UN "tweeters," that is, avid readers of the daily UN tweets. Some follow UN happenings that are livestreamed at: webtv.un.org. The Handmaids living in Paris had the opportunity to attend parallel events during the Paris UN Climate Change Summit (COP21) in 2015. As the Handmaid representative, I attend UN events in New York like the Indigenous Peoples' Forum and the Conference on the Status of Women. I have also invited Handmaids to take part in UN surveys to contribute their first-hand knowledge of local realities that help evaluate what is happening on the ground. The latest request, sent by email, came from the UN Indigenous Peoples' Forum:

> On behalf of Ms. Bas, the Director of the Division for Social Policy and Development, the Secretariat of the

> Permanent Forum on Indigenous Issues invites Institutions to complete the attached questionnaire on any action taken or planned related to the recommendations of the Permanent Forum on Indigenous Issues, implementation of the UN Declaration on the Rights of Indigenous Peoples and the outcome document of the World Conference on Indigenous People.

But the Handmaids, too, are changing in this evolving world of ours. Their membership reflects the global shift from Europe and the US to Latin America, Africa, and, above all, Asia. New ways are being found to engage in public theology in word and in action. Sisters are responding to the call to solidarity with the many displaced people across Syria and Iraq who are seeking safety from the advance of the Islamic State. One Handmaid has been working with the Jesuits in Dohuk, Kurdistan, 60 kilometers from the raging battle to retake Mosul from ISIS. Her regular chronicles have provided credible and heart-rending data and unending lists of martyrs among the *Peshmerga*.[13] Sisters are also asking for training to lobby politicians on behalf of the vulnerable and threatened at local level. In the Philippines, the Sisters have given their full support to the Bishops' anti-violence program, "Do Not Kill," in response to the extrajudicial killing of drug pushers. In the US, the Handmaids have issued the following post-election 2016 statement on their webpage:

> The Handmaids of the Sacred Heart of Jesus, grounded in the Gospel and the ACI mission, are committed, in this 'Divided States of America', to uphold the dignity of every person enshrined in the Constitution, and wish to work for the common good of our nation and to promote a living faith that works justice. In our society, deeply in need of mercy, the Handmaids, with our Eucharistic-reparative charism and our rich experience of multiculturality can be agents of reconciliation and dialogue.
>
> We will continue working to protect to the fullest extent of the law, undocumented immigrants and will

---

13. The *Peshmerga* are the military forces of the autonomous region of Iraqi Kurdistan.

support and stand in solidarity with all our brothers and sisters, regardless of their faith tradition, gender or culture, to preserve the religious freedoms on which this nation is founded.[14]

The Handmaids, like UNANIMA International and the UN, have also had a change of leadership, with the election of a new General Superior and her team. General Congregation XX in 2017 evaluated our ongoing commitment to social justice and the poor and also our participation in UNANIMA International. The Sisters, in preparation for the General Congregation, indicated a determination to look for new ways and opportunities to engage in public theology, because the list of social justice issues to be addressed is still long and urgent. The concerns are constant: human dignity, human rights, the common good, participation, solidarity, and all of them in the context of the pluralism and nationalism that characterizes society today. During that gathering, the Sisters renewed their commitment, individually and as a group, to support "people on the move" whether immigrants, refugees, displaced persons, or the victims of human trafficking.

What cannot and will not change is the Handmaids' commitment to the poor and their conviction that social justice and the Eucharist are inseparable. They believe that the suffering of the poor and oppressed is the paschal mystery that we celebrate daily in Eucharist. For the Sisters, the Eucharist is global and inclusive. It critiques exclusion and marginalization on any basis whatever. It offers a paradigm for reconciliation and an alternative language to that of war. It is about solidarity and caring. It is about real people, with faces and names. It is about the resources of the earth and basic human needs. It is an alternative narrative of history, read through the eyes of the losers and the disadvantaged: "The bottom billion."[15] It is about life, and quality of life lived to the full. It is about communion, dialogue, and sharing. It is about change

---

14. See: www.acjusa.org.

15. "The bottom billion" is a phrase much used. It was invented by the economist Paul Collier in his 2007 book of that title: *The Bottom Billion: Why the Poorer Countries are Failing and What To Do About It.*

and making the world a better place for everyone. Eucharist is the public expression of Christ's priorities. It is about ministry and public witness. As such, it critiques empire and greed. It unites voices passionate for global justice, due process, human rights, and compassion. Finally, for the Handmaids, Eucharist is essentially political and highly subversive.[16]

The Handmaids are continually challenged by the words of Pedro Arrupe, SJ: "When there is anyone hungry in the world, the Eucharist is incomplete everywhere in the world"[17] and the words of Raimundo Pannikar:

> The great challenge today is to convert the sacred bread into real bread, the liturgical peace into political peace, the worship of the Creator into reverence for the Creation, the Christian praying community into an authentic human fellowship. It is risky to celebrate Eucharist. We may have to leave it unfinished, having gone first to give back to the poor what belongs to them.[18]

I have shared our story so far. The next chapter is still in the mind and heart of God. It only remains for the Handmaids of the Sacred Heart to allow God to write it, with us and for us. That is what God did for Raphaela and the first Sisters, and he will do it for those who have come after them too.

As the Handmaids of the Sacred Heart move into the future, they will surely continue to weave their worship and their ministry into the theory and practice—the "what, why and how"—of public theology in countless, creative ways. They will always be gospel women in love with Jesus Christ, consecrated women involved in our global reality and in the United Nations, in Africa, Asia, Europe, Latin America, and the US—wherever God calls them to minister and to be. As disciples of Jesus, who identified himself with the poor and the vulnerable and who resisted the injustice of

16. Scott, passim.

17. Fr. Pedro Arrupe, SJ, at the 41st Eucharistic Congress in Philadelphia, 1975.

18. Pannikar, Raimundo. "Man as a Ritual Being." *Chicago Studies* 16 (1977) 27.

the religious and political powers of his own time, the Handmaids are committed to a similar subversive approach to social injustice. Public theology is who we are and what we do, our identity and our mission. The narrative continues.

Glossary

Accreditation at UN UN accreditation status is granted through the Economic and Social Council or the Department of Public Information and provides access to the UN.

Apostolic Letter A type of ecclesiastical document, which is issued by a pope.

Catholic Social Teaching The body of doctrine developed by the Catholic Church on matters of social justice, involving issues of poverty and wealth, economics, social organization, and the role of the state.

Charism In religious orders, charism describes the spiritual orientation and special characteristics of their mission given by God for the benefit of humanity.

Congregation A synonym for Order.

Constitutions The legislation of religious orders, sometimes call the Rule.

GLOSSARY

Declaration of Human Rights. Adopted by the UN General Assembly on December 10, 1948. The first global expression of the rights to which all human beings are entitled.

Economic and Social Council (ECOSOC) One of the six principal organs of the UN, responsible for coordinating the economic, social and related work of 15 UN specialized agencies.

Encyclical A papal letter concerning Catholic doctrine.

Eucharist The Catholic sacrament usually referred to as the Mass.

General Assembly One of the six principal organs of the United Nations, consisting of all the member states and the only one in which all member countries have equal representation. It is the main deliberative and policy-making body at the UN.

General Congregation The supreme decision-making body of a religious order consisting of elected representatives. It meets on a regular basis. Some orders refer to it as General Chapter.

Glossary

Handmaids of the Sacred Heart of Jesus	Religious Congregation founded by St. Raphaela Mary, of which the author is a member.
Human Rights	Commonly understood as inalienable, fundamental rights to which all human beings are entitled.
Ignatian Spirituality	Sometimes called Jesuit spirituality, founded on the spiritual experience of St. Ignatius of Loyola. Many women's religious apostolic orders have adopted it.
Institute	A synonym for Religious Order or Congregation.
Liberation Theology	A movement in Christian theology, developed mainly in the context of Latin America in the 1950s and 1960s. It emphasizes an integral mission, evangelization, and social responsibility.
Public Theology	The result of a growing need for theology to interact with public issues in contemporary society.
Non-governmental Organization	A not-for-profit organization that is independent from states and international governmental organizations.
Religious Women	Members of religious orders for women who profess the three vows of poverty, chastity, and obedience, and live in community.

Glossary

Religious Order The name, in Catholic tradition, for a group of men or women who profess the three vows of poverty, chastity, and obedience and live in community, following the spirit of a founder. Eg., Jesuits who live the spirituality of St. Ignatius.

RUN Acronym for "Religious at the UN," an organization for men and women members of religious orders who work in NGOs at the UN.

Secretary General The head of the United Nations Secretariat, one of the principal organs of the UN.

Security Council The most powerful body of the UN, with primary responsibility for maintaining international peace and security.

Sustainable Development Goals 17 aspirational goals and 139 targets adopted by the UN in 2015 to eradicate poverty and transform the world by 2030.

UNANIMA International An NGO with status at the UN, consisting of 21 orders of religious women.

United Nations An intergovernmental organization to promote international cooperation, peace, and security, founded after World War II.

GLOSSARY

United Nations Charter Foundational treaty of the United Nations, 1945.

United Nations Commission on Human Rights (UNCHR) A functional commission within the overall framework of the UN from 1946—2006.

United Nations Human Rights Council (UNHRC) Replaced the Human Rights Commission in 2006 as an inter-governmental agency in the UN whose 47 member states are responsible for promoting and protecting Human rights around the world.

Bibliography

ARTICLES

Barnett, Michael. "Humanitarianism Transformed." *Cambridge Core* 3 (2005) 723–40. https://doi.org/10,1017/S1537592705050401.

Berger, Julia. "Religious NGOs at the United Nations: Reflections on initial research and outstanding questions." https://www.academia.edu/7776173/Religious_NGOs_at_the_United_Nations_Reflections_on_initial_research_and_outstanding_questions.

Bostrom, Lisa. "Controversial Issues at the NGO Committee." csonet.org/content/documents/Controversialissues.pdf.

Freedman, Rosa. "The United Nations Human Rights Council: More of the Same." https//hosted.law.wisc.edu/worldpress/wilj/files/2014/01/Freedman_final_v2.pdf.

Gasser, Hans-Peter. "The United Nations and International Humanitarian Law: The International Committee of the Red Cross and the United Nations' Involvement in the implementation of international humanitarian law." Paper presented to the International Committee of the Red Cross, Geneva, (October 19–21, 1995). Httsp://www.icrc.org/resources/documents/misc/57jmuk.html.

Jacobsen, Eneida. "Models of Public Theology." *International Journal of Public Theology* 6 (2012) 7–22. www.academia.edu/6014390/Models_of_Public_Theology.

Lebovic, James H., and Eric Voeten. "The Politics of Shame: The Condemnation of Country Human Rights Practices in the UNCHR." *International Studies Quarterly* 50 (2006) 861–888. https://blogs.commons.georgetown.edu/erikvoeten/filres/2011/10/lesbolSQ.pdf.

Mannion, Gerard. "A Brief Genealogy of Public Theology, or Doing Theology when it Seems Nobody is Listening." *Annali di Studi Religiosi* 10 (2009) 121-154. KU Leuven.

Patrick, Stewart. "World Weary, Evaluating the United Nations at 70. What's Wrong with the United Nations." *Foreign Affairs* (2015). https://www.foreignaffairs.com/articles/2015-10-20/world-weary.

BIBLIOGRAPHY

Plesch, Dan. "How the United Nations Beat Hitler and Prepared the Peace." *Global Society* 22 (2008). https://www3.nccu.edu.tw/~lorenzo/How%20UN%Beat%Hitler%20and%20Prepared%20the%20Peace.pdf.
Schrijver, Nico. "The UN Human Rights Council: A New 'Society of the Committed' or just Old Wine in New Bottles?" *Leiden Journal of International Law* 20 (2007)809-13.
Weiss, Thomas G., et al. "The Third United Nations." *Global Governance* 15 (2017) 113-42. Journals.riener.com/doi/abs/10.5555/ggov2009.15.123.

BOOKS

Abbot, Walter M., SJ, ed. *The Documents of Vatican II*. Translated by Msgr. Joseph Gallagher. New York: America Press, 1966.
Ahern, Kevin, et al. *Public Theology and the Global Common Good: The Contribution of David Hollenbach*. Maryknoll, NY: Orbis, 2016.
Bloomquist, Karen L., ed. *Being the Church in the Midst of Empire: Trinitarian Reflections*. Theology in the Life of the Church 1. Minneapolis: Lutheran University Press, 2007.
———. *Theological Practices that Matter*. Theology in the Life of the Church 5. Minneapolis: Lutheran University Press, 2009.
Brueggemann, Walter. *Journey to the Common Good*. Louisville, KY: Westminster John Knox Press, 2010.
Crockett, William. *Eucharist: Symbol of Transformation*. Louisville, KY: Liturgical, 1989.
Fasulo, Linda. *An Insiders' Guide to the UN*. Newhaven, CT: Yale University Press, 2014.
Gutierrez, Gustavo. *Las Casa: In Search of the Poor of Jesus Christ*. Maryknoll, NY: Orbis, 1993.
Heyer, Kristin. *Prophetic and Public: The Social Witness of US Catholicism*. Washington, DC: Georgetown University Press, 2006.
Hollenbach, David. *The Global Face of Public Faith: Politics, Human Rights, and Christian Ethics*. Washington, DC: Georgetown University Press, 2003.
Lossky, Nicholas, et al., eds. *Dictionary of the Ecumenical Movement*. Geneva: WCC, 2002.
Marshall, Katherine and Saanen Marisa Van. *Development and Faith: Where Mind, Heart and Soul Work Together*. Washington, DC: World Bank, 2007.
Meisler, Stanley. *United Nations: A History*. New York: Grove, 1995.
Moltmann, Jurgen. *God for a Secular Society: The Public Relevance of Theology*. London: SCM, 1999.
Obiezu, Emeka. *It is Good for Us to be Here: Catholic Religious Institutes as NGOs at the United Nations*. Bloomington, IN: Xlibris, 2015.
Paeth, Scott R. *Exodus, Curch and Civil Society: Public Theology and Social Theory in the Work of Jurgen Moltmann*. Oxford: Routledge, 2016.
Sachs, Jeffrey. *The End of Poverty*, New York: Penguin, 2004.

Scott, Margaret. *The Eucharist and Social Justice*. New York: Paulist, 2009.
Storrar, William F., and Andrew R. Morton, eds. *Public Theology for the 21st Century: Essays in Honour of Duncan B. Forrester*. London: T& T Clark, 2004.
Tracy, David. *Analogical Imagination*. Quoted by T. Howland Sanks, SJ, in *Theological Studies* 54 (1993) 698-727. http://cdn.theologicalstudies.net/54/54.4/54.4.5.pdf.
―――. *Dialogue with the Other: Inter-Religious Dialogue*. Louvain: Peeters, 1990.
Weiss, Thomas G., et al. *The United Nations in Changing World Politics*. Boulder, CO: Westview, 2017.
Welch, Claude E., Jr., ed. *NGOs and Human Rights Promise and Performance*: Philadelphia: University of Pennsylvania Press, 2001.
Yañez, Inmaculada. *Cimientos Para un Edificio, Santa Rafaela Maria del Sagrado Corazon*. Madrid: BAC, 1979.
―――. *Hemos Creido En El Amor*. Rome: Esclavas del Sagrado Corazon, 1975.

CHURCH DOCUMENTS ONLINE

Benedict XVI. *Caritas in Veritate*. http://w2.vatican.va/content/benedict-xvi/en/encyclicals/documents/hf_ben-xvi_enc_20090629_caritas-in-veritate.
Bishops' Conference of UK. *Choosing The Common Good*. www.cbcew.org.uk/content/.../choosing-the-common-good-2010.pdf
Francis. *Gaudium Evangelii*. http://w2.vatican.va/content/francesco/en/apost_exhortations/documents/papa-francesco_esortazione-ap_20131.
―――. *Laudato Sí*. http://w2.vatican.va/content/francesco/en/encyclicals/documents/papa-francesco_20150524_enciclica-laudato-si.html.
John XXIII. *Mater et Magistra*. http://w2.vatican.va/content/john-xxiii/en/encyclicals/documents/hf_j-xxiii_enc_15051961_mater.html.
―――. *Pacem in Terris*. http://w2.vatican.va/content/john-xxiii/en/encyclicals/documents/hf_j-xxiii_enc_11041963_pacem.html.
John Paul II. *Centesimus Annus*. http://w2.vatican.va/content/john-paul-ii/en/encyclicals/documents/hf_jp-ii_enc_01051991_centesimus-annus.html.
―――. *Laborem Exercens*. http://w2.vatican.va/content/john-paul-ii/en/encyclicals/documents/hf_jp-ii_enc_14091981_laborem-exercens.html.
―――. *Sollicitudo Res Socialis (On Social Concerns)*. http://w2.vatican.va.content/john-paul-ii-/en/encyclicals/documents/hf_jp_iienc_30121987_sollicitudo-rei-socialis.htlm.
Leo XIII. *Rerum Novarum*. http:w2.vatican.va/contents/leo-xiii/en/encyclicals/documents/hf_l-xiii_en_15051891_rerum-novarum.htlm.
Paul VI. *Octogesima Adveniens*. http://w2.vatican.va/content/paul-vi/en/apost_letters/documents/hf_p-vi_apl_19710514_octogesima-adveniens.html.

BIBLIOGRAPHY

———. *Populorum Progressio.* http://w2.vatican.va/content/paul-vi/en/encyclicals/documents/hf_p-vi_enc_26031967_populorum.html.

Pius XI. *Quadragesimo Anno.* http://w2.vatican.va/content/pius-xi/en/encyclicals/documents/hf_p-xi_enc_19310515_quadragesimo-anno.html.

Pontifical Council for Justice and Peace. "Compendium of the Social Doctrine of the Church." https://www.vatican.va/roman_cuira/pontofical_council/justpeace/documents/rc_pc_justpeace_doc_20060526_compendio-dott-soc_en.htlm.

Vatican Council II. *Gaudium et Spes.* In *The Vatican Collection: The Conciliar and Postconciliar Documents,* vol. 1, edited by Austin Flannery, 903–1001. Northport, NY: Costello, 1996.

———. *Nostra Aetate.* http://www.vatican.va/archive/hist_councils/ii_vatican_council/documents/vat-ii_decl_19651028_nostra-aetate.

OTHER UNPUBLISHED DOCUMENTS

Handmaids of the Sacred Heart of Jesus. "Constitutions." Rome, 1983.
———. "General Congregation XI." Rome, 1969.
———. "General Congregation XII." Rome, 1977.
———. "General Congregation XIII." Rome, 1982.
———. "General Congregation XIV." Rome, 1987.
———. "General Congregation XV." Rome, 1992.
———. "General Congregation XVI." Rome, 1997.
———. "General Congregation XVII." Rome, 2002.
———. "General Congregation XVIII." Rome, 2007.
———. "General Congregation XIX." Rome, 2012.
UNANIMA International. "Board Members' Handbook."

www.ingramcontent.com/pod-product-compliance
Lightning Source LLC
Chambersburg PA
CBHW072152160426
43197CB00012B/2353